CliffsNotes™

Baldwi...

Go Tell I...
Mountain

By Sherry Ann McNett

IN THIS BOOK

- ■ Learn about the Life and Background of the Author
- ■ Preview an Introduction to the Novel
- ■ Study a graphical Character Map
- ■ Explore themes and literary devices in the Critical Commentaries
- ■ Examine in-depth Character Analyses
- ■ Enhance your understanding of the work with Critical Essays
- ■ Reinforce what you learn with CliffsNotes Review
- ■ Find additional information to further your study in CliffsNotes Resource Center and online at www.cliffsnotes.com

IDG Books Worldwide, Inc.
An International Data Group Company
Foster City, CA • Chicago, IL • Indianapolis, IN • New York, NY

About the Author

Sherry Ann McNett received her undergraduate degree at Ball State University and has taught English in South Korea and Brazil. She currently lives and works in Indiana.

Publisher's Acknowledgments

Editorial

Project Editor: Tracy Barr

Acquisitions Editor: Greg Tubach

Glossary Editors: The editors and staff at Webster's New World™ Dictionaries

Editorial Administrator: Michelle Hacker

Production

Indexer: York Production Services, Inc.

Proofreader: York Production Services, Inc.

IDG Books Indianapolis Production Department

CliffsNotes™ Baldwin's *Go Tell It on the Mountain*

Published by

IDG Books Worldwide, Inc.

An International Data Group Company

919 E. Hillsdale Blvd.

Suite 300

Foster City, CA 94404

www.idgbooks.com (IDG Books Worldwide Web site)
www.cliffsnotes.com (CliffsNotes Web site)

Library of Congress Catalog Card No.: 00-107803

ISBN: 0-7645-8649-1

Printed in the United States of America

10 9 8 7 6 5 4 3 2 1

1O/RR/RS/QQ/IN

Distributed in the United States by IDG Books Worldwide, Inc.

Distributed by CDG Books Canada Inc. for Canada; by Transworld Publishers Limited in the United Kingdom; by IDG Norge Books for Norway; by IDG Sweden Books for Sweden; by IDG Books Australia Publishing Corporation Pty. Ltd. for Australia and New Zealand; by TransQuest Publishers Pte Ltd. for Singapore, Malaysia, Thailand, Indonesia, and Hong Kong; by Gotop Information Inc. for Taiwan; by ICG Muse, Inc. for Japan; by Norma Comunicaciones S.A. for Columbia; by Intersoft for South Africa; by Eyrolles for France; by International Thomson Publishing for Germany, Austria and Switzerland; by Distribuidora Cuspide for Argentina; by LR International for Brazil; by Galileo Libros for Chile; by Ediciones ZETA S.C.R. Ltda. for Peru; by WS Computer Publishing Corporation, Inc., for the Philippines; by Contemporanea de Ediciones for Venezuela; by Express Computer Distributors for the Caribbean and West Indies; by Micronesia Media Distributor, Inc. for Micronesia; by Grupo Editorial Norma S.A. for Guatemala; by Chips Computadoras S.A. de C.V. for Mexico; by Editorial Norma de Panama S.A. for Panama; by American Bookshops for Finland. Authorized Sales Agent: Anthony Rudkin Associates for the Middle East and North Africa.

For general information on IDG Books Worldwide's books in the U.S., please call our Consumer Customer Service department at **800-762-2974**. For reseller information, including discounts and premium sales, please call our Reseller Customer Service department at **800-434-3422**.

For information on where to purchase IDG Books Worldwide's books outside the U.S., please contact our International Sales department at **317-596-5530** or fax **317-572-4002**.

For consumer information on foreign language translations, please contact our Customer Service department at **1-800-434-3422**, fax **317-572-4002**, or e-mail rights@idgbooks.com.

For information on licensing foreign or domestic rights, please phone **+1-650-653-7098**.

For sales inquiries and special prices for bulk quantities, please contact our Order Services department at **800-434-3422** or write to the address above.

For information on using IDG Books Worldwide's books in the classroom or for ordering examination copies, please contact our Educational Sales department at **800-434-2086** or fax **317-572-4005**.

For press review copies, author interviews, or other publicity information, please contact our Public Relations department at **650-653-7000** or fax **650-653-7500**.

For authorization to photocopy items for corporate, personal, or educational use, please contact Copyright Clearance Center, 222 Rosewood Drive, Danvers, MA 01923, or fax **978-750-4470**.

Table of Contents

How to Use This Book

CliffsNotes Baldwin's *Go Tell It on the Mountain* supplements the original work, giving you background information about the author, an introduction to the novel, a graphical character map, critical commentaries, expanded glossaries, and a comprehensive index. CliffsNotes Review tests your comprehension of the original text and reinforces learning with questions and answers, practice projects, and more. For further information on James Baldwin and *Go Tell It on the Mountain*, check out the CliffsNotes Resource Center.

CliffsNotes provides the following icons to highlight essential elements of particular interest:

Reveals the underlying themes in the work.

Helps you to more easily relate to or discover the depth of a character.

Uncovers elements such as setting, atmosphere, mystery, passion, violence, irony, symbolism, tragedy, foreshadowing, and satire.

Enables you to appreciate the nuances of words and phrases.

Don't Miss Our Web Site

Discover classic literature as well as modern-day treasures by visiting the CliffsNotes Web site at www.cliffsnotes.com. You can obtain a quick download of a CliffsNotes title, purchase a title in print form, browse our catalog, or view online samples.

You'll also find interactive tools that are fun and informative, links to interesting Web sites, tips, articles, and additional resources to help you, not only for literature, but for test prep, finance, careers, computers, and the Internet too. See you at www.cliffsnotes.com!

LIFE AND BACKGROUND OF THE AUTHOR

Early Years and Education

James Baldwin was born the illegitimate son of Emma Berdis Jones on August 2, 1924, in Harlem Hospital. In James's third year, his mother married the Reverend David Baldwin, a fire and brimstone lay preacher, who legally adopted James.

James attended Public School 24 in Harlem, where he met a young white teacher named Orilla Miller. Nicknamed "Bill" by the young Baldwin, Miller was to have a profound effect on Baldwin's life. She directed his first play and encouraged his talents. The two discussed literature and went to museums together. Miller even won David Baldwin's permission to take James to the theater, an activity strictly forbidden by the elder Baldwin. Later, James was to give credit to Bill for her lack of racism. He explained that it was "certainly partly because of her, who arrived in my terrifying life so soon, that I never really managed to hate white people."

After elementary school, Baldwin went on to Frederic Douglas Junior high. It was here that he met Countee Cullen (an American poet) and Herman W. Porter, both of whom were teachers at the school during the years that Baldwin attended, and both would have a lasting impact on his life. Cullen encouraged James to participate in the school's literary club, which he was the founder and advisor of. Baldwin was enchanted by Cullen's warmth and openness, and soon Cullen became a father figure to the troubled and lonely youth.

Porter was in charge of *The Douglas Pilot*, the school magazine, and made Baldwin the editor of the publication to which he would also contribute. Porter introduced James to the public library and taught him how to overcome the racial slurs and hostility that he sometimes encountered there. These two teachers and role models had a profound impact on Baldwin's life by showing him that black men could be successful, educated, and strong.

In the summer of 1938, James experienced a religious conversion and began preaching. Standing in the pulpit, he was overcome with a sense of wonder and power in the art of rhetoric. The speaking skills that he developed as a minister would later serve him well in his vocation as a writer. More immediately, however, James found that his position as minister gave him power at home. He soon began to openly defy his father, who was forced to surrender now that his son was also a member of the ministry. For instance, when David suggested that

James find a job and quit school, the younger Baldwin refused, opting to continue on to high school.

Luckily James had taken the advice of Countee Cullen and applied for admittance to the prestigious De Witt Clinton High School, from which scores of successful and famous people had graduated. His classmates were mainly white, but they came from liberal families who were more interested in James's talent than his skin tone. Here he formed close ties with other students with whom he worked on *The Magpie*, the school's newspaper.

At 16, James left the ministry because of what he perceived as hypocrisy and racism, which had destroyed his faith in the church. This split had its beginnings when James met Beauford Delany. A mutual friend had introduced the two at a point when James was very depressed and confused. Delany, an artist, was perhaps the most influential person in Baldwin's life. He introduced the young man to music, took him to galleries, taught Baldwin to think like an artist, and showed him that it was possible to make a living at it.

Early Career and Writing

After graduation, Baldwin found it necessary to find full time employment so that he could support himself. He moved in with a friend but was forced to return home when he was fired from his job. When he returned home, he found his mother pregnant and his father in the hospital due to his deteriorating mental capacity. The last Baldwin baby, Paula, was born on July 29, 1943. It was on the same day that his father passed away. James and Beuford scraped together enough money for a funeral service, held on James's birthday.

Baldwin continued to live at home in an attempt to support his family but was unable to keep a job. Resentment at his responsibilities to his family precluding the chance of his success as a writer became unbearable. He moved out and found work in Greenwich Village. A restaurant owner named Connie Williams, who was sympathetic to Baldwin's plight, took the young man under her wing and employed him as a waiter. She often let him stay at her apartment and gave him food for his family.

During this period, Baldwin met many artists and writers who frequented William's restaurant. He also began his search for his sexual identity by having a number of one-night affairs with men but also continuing to have relationships with women. He met and fell in love with a man named Eugene Worth. Afraid of loosing a friendship by revealing his true feelings, Baldwin never expressed his love. Unfortunately, Worth committed suicide by jumping off the George Washington Bridge after making an oblique comment about the possibility that he was in love with Baldwin. James never recovered from the loss of his friend.

It was also during this time that Baldwin began to write seriously. A young woman who had been impressed by Baldwin's reading of his manuscript *In My Father's House* (a precursor to *Go Tell It on the Mountain*) introduced him to the American novelist Richard Wright. Wright was also impressed with the work of the younger man and helped to secure for him a Eugene F. Saxon Foundation Fellowship. The fellowship, which included $500, was awarded to Baldwin in November of 1945. Unfortunately, *In My Father's House* was not deemed worthy of being published, and Baldwin was depressed and fearful that he had not lived up to the Wright's expectations.

In 1947, Baldwin was finally published professionally; however, it wasn't a novel but a book review that launched his writing career. This book review was followed by a number of essays. His first work of fiction was published in October of 1948. A proposed project with a photographer friend about Harlem churches won Baldwin a Rosenwald fellowship. Though the project was never completed, it did give Baldwin the money needed to make his long dreamed of trip to Paris. Ironically, it was in Paris that Baldwin came to understand himself, his homeland, and his culture.

Although an expatriate writer, Baldwin remained active in events that shaped American culture. He divided his time between Europe and the United States, and his role in the Civil Rights movement cannot be overlooked. He met with Martin Luther King, Jr., Malcolm X, Medgar Evers, and a host of other politically active notables in an effort to bring about constructive social change. His beliefs on race and race relations would color many of his novels and inspire a large percentage of his essays.

Major Literary Works

Baldwin was a proficient writer. He produced scores of reviews, essays, plays, short stories, and novels. The following is a short list of what is widely regarded as his most important works and a short description of their content or significance.

Baldwin wrote "Everybody's Protest Novel" (1949) shortly after his arrival in Paris. The essay attacked the ideology traditionally found in protest novels. Many, including Richard Wright, saw the article as a personal attack on Wright and his works. Not surprisingly, this caused a rift, but not a break, in the friendship between the two authors.

Go Tell It on the Mountain, which Baldwin had worked on for years under various titles, was finally finished during a trip to Switzerland. When New York publisher Alfred Knopf expressed interest in publishing the work, Baldwin returned to America on a ticked bought with a loan from Marlon Brando. His novel was published a year later in 1953 and received rave reviews.

It was in Paris that his next work, *The Amen Corner* (1954), was published. A novel about a young man who leaves his home and church to become a musician and find himself can be seen as a continuation of *Mountain* and, like his previous novel, is partially autobiographical.

Notes of a Native Son (1955), a collection of Baldwin's essays from 1948 to 1955, was his next major work. Some pieces like "Everybody's Protest Novel" had been previously published, but others were seen for the first time in this publication.

Giovanni's Room (1956) tells the story of David, an American living in Paris who falls in love with an Italian bartender named Giovanni. In an attempt to deny the true nature of his sexuality, the protagonist proposes to an American girl and leaves Giovanni, who, jilted, commits a murder and is executed. The woman leaves David when it becomes clear that their relationship is a failure, and David returns to his past life, full of anguish for his lost Giovanni. Baldwin was nervous before the publication of this novel because he saw that, with its publication, he would no longer be able to hide the fact of his own homosexuality from his family, and he feared their rejection.

"Sonny's Blues" (1957) is the story of two brothers. Sonny is a musician who is also a heroin addict. His brother, instilled with a feeling of responsibility for his sibling by their mother, tries to understand Sonny and his addiction.

Another Country (1962) tells the story of a Jazz musician who is deeply hurt by racism and thus unable to trust anyone and so unable to give or accept love.

Tell Me How Long the Train's Been Gone (1968) tells the tale of a young man from Harlem and his rise to fame as an actor. It chronicles the events of his life and his struggles with his sexuality and lovers.

The relationship between two lovers and their families is the focus of *If Beale Street Could Talk* (1974). The novel concerns the hypocrisy found in the church and relationships between family members—especially sisters, who for the first time make a serious appearance in Baldwin's work.

In *Just Above My Head* (1979), the narrator, Hal, tells the story of a dearly loved brother and a happy childhood. The Millers, friends of Hal's family, were not so lucky. Mrs. Miller died when their daughter Julia, a successful child-preacher, was 14 years old. To escape her brutal and sexually abusive father, Julia becomes a prostitute. Through a seemingly endless string of trials, Hal and Julia settle down in neighboring towns to enjoy middle age and middle class. It is one of Baldwin's sermons on the importance of choosing love over security.

Later Years

During the 1980's, Baldwin taught classes at the University of Amherst. His courses included a history of the Civil Rights movement and classes on expatriate writers like himself.

In addition to living in Paris, Baldwin also spent time in Switzerland and Istanbul and traveled to Africa and the Soviet Union. It was in St. Paul de Vence that Baldwin was first diagnosed with esophageal cancer. He passed away on November 30, 1987, surrounded by family and loving friends.

Awards

Throughout his life, Baldwin was recognized not only for his achievements in literature but also for his work in the Civil Rights struggle and for his efforts to facilitate understanding and respect between all people. Private institutions, public organizations, and government agencies all chose to honor him in their own ways:

1945   Eugene F. Saxon Fellowship

1948   Rosenwald Fellowship

1954   Guggenheim Fellowship and the MacDowell Colony Fellowship

1956   Partisan Review Fellowship and a grant from the National Institute of Arts and Letters

1959   Ford Foundation Grant

1961   Certificate of Recognition from the National Conference on Christians and Jews

1963   George Polk Memorial Award

1964   Honorary Degree from City University of New York

1965   Martin Luther King Memorial medal and an Honorary Degree from the University of Massachusetts

1981   Best Nonfiction Award from *Playboy* Magazine

1982   French Legion of Honor from Francois Mitterrand

INTRODUCTION TO THE NOVEL

Introduction

Go Tell It on the Mountain is a multifaceted novel that tells many different stories and confronts many different themes. On the simplest level, it is the story of a young boy coming of age. The boy's story gains complexity as it is interwoven with the stories of his mother, father, and aunt. *Go Tell It on the Mountain* is also the story of religion and racism and familial expectations and perceptions and how these forces impact people struggling to survive.

Style of Narration

Go Tell It on the Mountain doesn't follow what many would consider to be the standard style of narration in which the events in the novel are presented sequentially and move, as the characters do, through a semblance of real time. Instead, *Go Tell It on the Mountain* is set on the birthday of John Grimes, but the story spans several decades. The flashbacks of John's aunt, his mother, and his father give the reader insight into the lives and minds of the characters.

Such insight was important to Baldwin who was most interested in the person behind the persona. He believed that to truly know a person and to understand why a person reacts or behaves in a certain way, you have to know the important events that shaped that person's life. By the end of the novel, the manner in which the characters react to any given situation can be extrapolated not only from their past actions but also by the understanding that the reader has gained of the character's motivating force.

By using the frame story, Baldwin is able to tell many stories in such a way that the readers essentially go on a voyage of discovery, learning about the characters as they are revealed by themselves and by the others. Had Baldwin told the story in traditional linear style, much of the impact would have been lost. By withholding key information and surprising the reader with it throughout the novel, Baldwin builds suspense and is better able to hold the interest of his audience.

This style of narration also imitates the way people learn about each other in real life. Upon first meeting, a person does not truly understand the motivation behind another person's actions. In the novel, for example, the reader cannot comprehend the actions and reactions of the characters in Part One because so very little is known about them. By reading through, though, the reader gains an understanding of the characters and the events that shaped their lives and, therefore, gains an understanding of why they behave as they do.

Baldwin believed that the only way to happiness was to truly know the people in one's life. *In Go Tell It on the Mountain*, it is painfully obvious that none of the characters really know each other. It is only the omniscient narrator who has a full and unbiased knowledge of all events of significant importance. The use of the omniscient narrator is, in itself, vital to the novel because no single character knows the full and true story of every other character. In fact, the individual characters cannot be trusted to give an accurate description of their own personal histories, colored as these histories are by their own feelings and perceptions.

By using the omniscient narrator, Baldwin is able to give an accurate and complete description of the lives of his characters. The reader is shown their emotions, actions, and reactions and is therefore able to understand their personalities. Although individual characters may interpret and react to the same situation in different ways according to their own preconceptions and prejudices, the reader is given the opportunity to see events as they actually happened.

Historical Context

Go Tell It on the Mountain is set during the Great Migration, a time in American history characterized by a mass exodus of African Americans from the rural south to northern cities. In the years between 1916 and 1921, half a million southern blacks (representing 5 percent of the black population) moved to northern and, to a lesser extent, western cities. In a broader historical context, which includes the time period between 1890–1960, the statistics are even more startling. In 1890, 90 percent of American blacks lived in southern and rural settings, while the remaining 10 percent lived in northern or urban settings. By 1960, those statistics had reversed, with 90 percent of African Americans living outside the South and in urban settings.

The Chicago Defender, a northern newspaper, encouraged the migration by advertising jobs and promising better opportunities in the North than could be found in the South. Many factory owners offered to pay the train fare for southern blacks, who agreed, in return, to work for these factory owners until the price of the ticket could be deducted from the workers' pay. Many southerners were encouraged by *The Chicago Defender* in this way to travel north. In fact, the *Defender* was so effective in drawing people to the North that it was banned in several southern counties by whites who saw their cheap labor pool disappearing.

Many people were ready to leave the South for a variety of reasons: a weak agricultural system that offered low wages and back-breaking work and little chance for advancement; repressive Jim Crow laws and a legal system that offered little outlet for social protest; and, in the years between 1900 to 1910, the highest number of lynchings in America's history. Those years experienced a record 846 reported lynchings. Of those, 754 were of blacks.

In the novel, the reader can see that the Great Migration is underway. There are many characters who travel north during the story. The first, of whom the reader is only shown a brief glimpse, is the father of Florence and Gabriel. In fact, the only information Florence tells about him is that he went North. "And not only her Father; every day she heard that another man or woman had said farewell to this iron earth and sky, and started on the journey north." Florence herself is the next to make the journey, followed by Ester. Later, Ester's grown son follows his mother's footsteps and dies in Chicago. Elizabeth and Richard move to New York to start their lives together. Gabriel, the last character to move north, brings the count to seven.

A Brief Synopsis

The first section of the novel begins on the birthday of John Grimes, the protagonist. John begins his day by entering the kitchen where his mother, Elizabeth, and younger brother, Roy, are arguing about Gabriel, the boys' father. Roy is upset because he doesn't feel that he has the type of relationship with his father that he should. Gabriel is distant, and his children do not feel comfortable talking to him; he is also brutal, beating his children for their transgressions. After John finishes his breakfast and Elizabeth sends him to clean the front room of their home, John is understandably upset because no one has remembered his birthday.

As John finishes sweeping and dusting, Elizabeth gives him money so that he can buy himself something for his birthday. John sets out into the city. His first stop is Central Park and then Broadway, where he decides to see a movie, an activity forbidden by his strictly religious father.

Upon returning home, John learns that Roy has been stabbed. Gabriel, who is treating Roy's wound with uncharacteristic gentleness, turns his anger upon Elizabeth, blaming the boys' mother for Roy's wild ways. Despite the attempt of Gabriel's sister, Florence, to talk reasonably to Gabriel and to protect Elizabeth, Gabriel strikes his wife. The blow enrages Roy who, in trying to protect his mother, also receives a beating from Gabriel.

The next scene finds John and Elisha, John's friend and youth minister, cleaning the church that the family attends. They complete their work in time for Saturday evening Tarry Service. John is not surprised to see his mother and father enter the church, but he is surprised to see that his aunt has accompanied them.

Part Two, "The Prayers of the Saints," begins with "Florence's Prayer." Florence kneels at the altar, trying to remember how to pray. Her thoughts stray back to her childhood and the bitterness that she felt towards Gabriel because, being a boy and their mother's favorite, he was given everything their mother could afford. Despite all the sacrifices made by his mother and all of the deprivations suffered by Florence for his good, Gabriel wasted his education and continually caused trouble in and around town. As Gabriel grew, so did his vices. Playing hooky and causing mischief turned into drinking and gambling. Finally Florence had had enough. She bought a train ticket to New York City, said goodbye to her dying mother and bewildered brother, and left.

In New York, Florence married Frank, mistakenly believing that she could control him. After an evening of especially bitter arguing, Frank walked out, never to return. Florence learned much later from the woman Frank had moved in with that he had been killed oversees during WWI and was buried in France.

Back in the present, Florence hears Gabriel's voice, which triggers thoughts of her childhood friend and Gabriel's first wife, Deborah. Many years ago, Florence had received a letter from Deborah, telling of Deborah's suspicions of Gabriel's infidelity. Deborah believed that Gabriel had had an affair and fathered a child whom he had not claimed as his own. Florence advised Deborah to confront Gabriel with her suspicions and now wonders if she ever did. Florence carries the letter in her purse, hoping that she will live long enough to use the letter to bring about Gabriel's destruction. She becomes suddenly angry with God that she is dying while her brother is allowed to live and that their dead mother will see her fall into Hell. Florence begins to weep.

In "Gabriel's Prayer," Gabriel hears his sister's cry and is taken back to the morning he was saved: Dragging himself home after a night of drinking and carousing, Gabriel fell to the ground and experienced a religious conversion. He began preaching, and after his mother's death, the neighbor Deborah began to look after him, cooking his meals and mending his clothes.

There was to be a large revival meeting during which 24 widely known and well-respected ministers would meet and take turns preaching. To his surprise and honor, Gabriel was invited to be one of their number. On the final night, a banquet was held during which one of the elder ministers mocked Deborah for her rape (which occurred when she was 16) and her now chaste life. Much offended, Gabriel chastised the man for his lack of discretion. That evening Gabriel had two dreams that he interpreted to mean that God intended for him to marry Deborah. She tearfully accepted his proposal.

Cries from Elisha, who lies prone on the floor in religious ecstasy, revive Gabriel from his memories. Gabriel, for a moment, thinks that it is John on the floor. When he sees that it is not, he is relieved but also bitter that neither of his own sons are in the church with him: Roy is at home wounded and angry, and the other child (Royal, whom Gabriel never claimed as his son) is dead. Again Gabriel recalls the past.

Soon after Gabriel first began to preach, Ester came to town with her mother and stepfather. Gabriel saw Ester as sinful because every day after work a different boy escorted Ester home. One day, Gabriel invited Ester to church on a night that he was to speak. To everyone's surprise, Ester and her mother attended the service that evening. Gabriel preached a powerful sermon, one destined to be remembered for many years to come. Nevertheless, Gabriel was angered when his words did not draw Ester from her seat and to the altar to ask for God's forgiveness and mercy. Soon after this episode, Ester and Gabriel had a short-lived affair during which Ester became pregnant. When she told Gabriel of her condition, he initially denied that the child was his and only agreed to help her after she threatened to tell the community of his indiscretion. He gave Ester money that he stole from Deborah, and Ester left for Chicago to have the baby. Ester died in childbirth. Her body, as well as the newborn Royal, was brought back by her grieving mother. Gabriel never claimed the boy as his own. Many years later, Deborah told him that Royal had been stabbed and killed in a fight over a game of cards. Gabriel finally admitted to Deborah that Royal was indeed his child.

In "Elizabeth's Prayer," Elizabeth recalls her childhood and how she came to be where she is: Elizabeth was not very close to her mother, but she adored her father. After her mother's death, Elizabeth's maternal aunt took her away from her father, claiming that he was incapable of raising a little girl. Elizabeth never felt loved by her aunt and was very unhappy growing up in her aunt's home.

One summer, Elizabeth met Richard, who was working as a clerk in a local store. Soon the two developed a relationship and planned to marry. They went to New York together where they both found work in the same hotel. Their happiness continued until Richard was arrested for a crime he did not commit. Although finally found not guilty of the charge, Richard committed suicide out of shame and humiliation. Elizabeth never had the chance to tell him that she was pregnant with his child.

Elizabeth met Florence when they were both working as cleaning women in the same office building. Both women shunned the company of others but managed to become friends. Florence introduced Elizabeth to Gabriel shortly after his arrival in the city. Gabriel was very kind to Elizabeth and the infant John. Despite Florence's objections, the two were soon married.

Elizabeth is brought back to the present by a cry from John. He is lying on the floor overcome by the power of the Holy Ghost.

In Part Three, "The Threshing Floor," John's story is told. Without knowing how he came to be there, John is aware that he is lying on the church floor. He tries to rise but finds himself unable to stand. He experiences several visions culminating in a brief glimpse of God and his rebirth into a new and holy life. After rising, John approaches Gabriel, hoping that his experience will bring the two of them together. It has just the opposite effect, however, causing even more bitterness and resentment in Gabriel.

As the members of the church depart for home, Florence confronts Gabriel with Deborah's letter and her knowledge of his illegitimate son. Gabriel claims that he has been forgiven by God and refuses to respond to his sister's accusations. Florence promises to make the truth known to Elizabeth and leaves for home.

Elisha and John, who are walking together, stop outside John's house. Elisha gives John a few parting words of encouragement and advice and also departs. John speaks words full of hope for the future.

List of Characters

John Grimes   The novel's main character. The novel tells of his personal struggles and his coming of age in a strict, religious atmosphere.

Gabriel Grimes   John's stepfather. Much of the novel centers on John's struggle with Gabriel and their mutual lack of understanding.

Elizabeth Grimes   John's mother and Gabriel's wife. Elizabeth accepts her life in Gabriel's shadow because of her past misfortunes and her desire for redemption. Although a source of comfort, she is a constant puzzle to John because of her silence.

Florence   John's aunt and Gabriel's sister. Paradoxically, Florence in many ways serves as a protector even though she often fails in that role.

Roy   Gabriel and Elizabeth's son and John's half-brother. Although he is Gabriel's favored son, the boy's wild nature often causes problems not only for himself but also for his mother and brother.

Royal   Gabriel's illegitimate son who was conceived during a short affair with Ester. Memories of Royal and his own lack of involvement in the boy's life haunt Gabriel throughout his own life and color his relationships with his other children.

Ester   Gabriel's mistress who died giving birth to his son Royal. Memories of Ester are a reminder to Gabriel of the consequences of sin and the ease of falling from the path of the righteous.

Elisha   The youth minister and piano player at the Church of the Fire Baptized. He is John's friend and advisor.

Deborah   Gabriel's first wife. She appears in the memories of Gabriel and Florence but is dead at the time in which the current action takes place.

Elizabeth's aunt Sister of Elizabeth's mother. She separated Elizabeth from her father and took her to live with her in Maryland after the death of Elizabeth's mother.

Richard Elizabeth's first love and the biological father of John. He committed suicide before learning of Elizabeth's pregnancy.

Rachel Florence and Gabriel's mother who was born in slavery and lost several other children.

Frank Florence's husband who deserted her and later died in WWI.

Sister McDonald Ester's mother.

Ruth and Sara Gabriel and Elizabeth's daughters. They are John's half-sisters.

Father James, Deacon Braithwaite, Ella Mae, Sister McCandless, Praying Mother Washington Members of the Church of the Fire Baptized.

Character Map

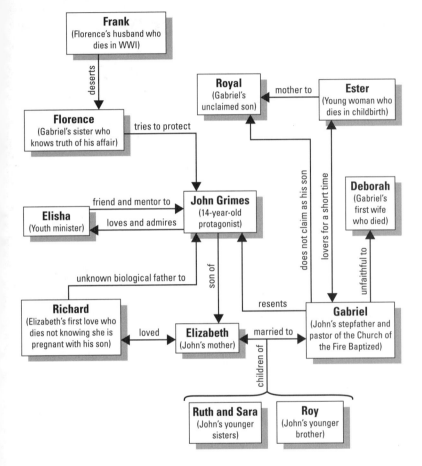

Frank
(Florence's husband who dies in WWI)

deserts

Florence
(Gabriel's sister who knows truth of his affair)

tries to protect

Royal
(Gabriel's unclaimed son)

mother to

Ester
(Young woman who dies in childbirth)

friend and mentor to

John Grimes
(14-year-old protagonist)

Elisha
(Youth minister)

loves and admires

does not claim as his son

lovers for a short time

Deborah
(Gabriel's first wife who died)

unknown biological father to

son of

resents

unfaithful to

Richard
(Elizabeth's first love who dies not knowing she is pregnant with his son)

loved

Elizabeth
(John's mother)

married to

Gabriel
(John's stepfather and pastor of the Church of the Fire Baptized)

children of

Ruth and Sara
(John's younger sisters)

Roy
(John's younger brother)

CRITICAL
COMMENTARIES

Part One: The Seventh Day

Summary

The novel begins in New York City on the 14th birthday of the central character in the plot, John Grimes. The reader is told immediately that the people in John's life all expect him to become a preacher when he comes of age, just as his father did. John's memories reveal bittersweet Sunday mornings as the Grimes family prepares for church services that are held in a store front church called "The Temple of the Fire Baptized," which is just a few blocks up the street.

Despite expectations for John's future in the ministry, he is not the best Sunday school student. He often becomes distracted, forgets his lessons, and is reprimanded by his Sunday school teacher, Elisha, an older boy of 17 whom John greatly admires. While John's lapses bring him the anger of his father, his brother Roy's utter disinterest is generally expected, and "[e]veryone was always praying that the Lord would change Roy's heart." John is expected to be a good example to his younger brother.

Although church services at first appear to be very free, emotional, and spontaneous, there are strict standards and expectations that must not be violated. One Sunday, Father James calls Elisha and Ella Mae before the congregation and reprimands them for the time that they have been spending together, warning them against "the sin he knew they had not committed yet," "a sin beyond all forgiveness."

The first of his family or his neighbors to wake that Saturday morning, John is greeted by a silent house. He feels an immediate sense of foreboding and recalls that he has sinned. His thoughts jump to wondering if his birthday will again go unremembered and uncelebrated.

John falls back asleep with his thoughts and awakens again after his father, Gabriel, has left for work. He goes to the kitchen to join his family and sees, as though for the first time, what the room really looks like: immured in dirt and poverty. His entrance interrupts an argument his mother and Roy, his brother, are having, and he is intensely disappointed to see that no special breakfast has been prepared to celebrate his birthday. The argument, about Gabriel and what kind of father and man he is, continues, and we see that it is one that Roy and Elizabeth have had before. Elizabeth defends her husband on the grounds that he is a good provider, while Roy derides him for beating his children. Despite the serious subject, the argument ends on a light note, and Elizabeth sends her sons off to do their weekly cleaning chores.

John's duty is to clean the front room, mainly to sweep the decaying rug in the front parlor—a Sisyphean task that John detests, because all his labor brings such a small reward and no personal satisfaction of accomplishment for him. The rug is perpetually dirty. When he has finished with the rug, John starts wiping dust from the mirror. In the midst of cleaning, he sees his own face and is shocked to see that he has not changed. He tries to see himself as his father does. He tries to find the features of the devil on his own face, those that his father has told him time and time again are there.

Giving up on trying to discover himself in his features, John reviews the family's possessions on the mantel. A malevolent green metal serpent sits in the midst of family photos and greeting cards. A photo of his father taken long ago in the South where Gabriel and his sister grew up reminds John that this is not his father's first marriage and makes him realize that, if Gabriel's first wife had lived, it would have negated John's entire existence. John wishes that he could ask this long dead woman, whom he believes Gabriel had loved, how he, John, could win his father's love.

John is called to the kitchen where his mother is doing laundry. To his surprise, she gives him money so that he can buy himself something for his birthday. He chooses to go to the movies, an activity forbidden by his father and, upon returning home, is told that his brother has been stabbed.

Although there is a great deal of blood, it is immediately obvious that Roy is in no mortal danger. While tender with Roy, Gabriel lashes out at Elizabeth verbally and then physically. After Roy calls his father a "black bastard" for slapping his mother, Gabriel removes his belt and beats Roy until Florence, the boys' aunt and Gabriel's sister, stops him.

John opens the church to clean before Saturday night Tarry Service and is shortly joined by Elisha, John's friend and youth minister, who has come to help him. The two argue playfully and then wrestle, a match that, for the first time, ends in a draw. Elisha speaks to John about salvation and foregoing earthly pleasures for the promise of Heaven. John is warned against sin and is urged to ask for the help of Jesus to overcome the devil. Soon other members of the congregation begin to arrive. John sees his parents and aunt walk in. He is shocked because he has never seen Florence in that church before and wonders what other strange happenings the night will bring.

Commentary

The title of this section has certain thematic significance: "The Seventh Day" is a biblical allusion referring to Genesis 2, verses 1–3: "And on the seventh day God ended his work which he had made; and he rested on the seventh day from all his work which he had made. And God blessed the seventh day and sanctified it. . . ." The biblical seventh day is a respite and a day of reward, a holy day of celebration and rest from the previous days' work in which God had completed his creation, and "God saw every thing that he had made, and, behold, it was *very* good."

Literary Device

Baldwin uses this creation-birth-rebirth image throughout the novel: The novel opens in March, the beginning of spring, associated with new life and birth. It is John's 14th birthday, "birthday" itself suggesting some significance in this regard and the special significance of the 14th birthday connoting puberty, that is, the end of childhood and the beginning of adulthood. Elizabeth, John's mother, is pregnant. The home and church pressure "unit[e] to drive [John] to the alter," that is, drive him to "being saved" or "born again." Perhaps most significantly, the image can be seen in the symbolic new beginning that virtually every adult character in the novel seeks in moving from the oppression of the South in search of something better in the North. The image appears even in the title of the novel; the "It" in *Go Tell It on the Mountain* is "Jesus Christ is born."

In the Christian world, Sunday has been designated as the symbolic representation of the seventh day, the Sabbath, the day that Christians have set aside as a day of rest to worship and to celebrate their religion. The allusion is certainly significant here in at least two ways. First, according to the Bible, God rested on the seventh day after his crowning creation—that of man—on the sixth day. Poignantly, it is on the sixth day, a Saturday, that John, one of the major characters, is fated to end his own childhood (innocence) and initiate the biological process of becoming a male adult—symbolically the physical creation of a man. As we will learn in the climax of the novel (Part Three, "The

Threshing Floor"), John will also end his religious dilemma and questioning and initiate the religious process of rebirth, symbolically creating a new Christian soul. The process of creation at least for that part of his life ends, and, when his life is taken up again the next day, John is changed and redefined.

Second, the mood, tone, and atmosphere of the Genesis creation serve as direct contrasts to the world that Baldwin describes in this section. When God created man on the sixth day, he gave him "dominion . . . over every living thing that moveth upon the earth," and when he surveyed his creation, God concluded "it was *very* good." The mood and tone are triumphant, hopeful, proud, and glorious. There is anticipation of great accomplishments and power for God's favorite and most significant creation in a bright, new, and clean world. This, however, is hardly the world or fortune of the Baldwin characters and, especially, of Baldwin's new man, John, who essentially has dominion over nothing and survives in a world that he views as filthy and sinful.

The opening vignettes represent the various settings—home, church, neighborhood—as dingy, drab, depressing, nearly worn out, and poverty laden. It presents the various characters—family, passersby, congregation, ministers, and authority figures—as oppressed and manipulated, highly sexual and emotional, and driven by reacting to circumstances rather than controlling (having dominion over) them. These descriptions conform to and exemplify the dirt imagery that Baldwin links to the story's general environment. These images communicate, at different times, various meanings from filthy or squalid conditions to contemptible or vile acts to personal corruption and sin. For example, consider the scene in which John surveys the family kitchen. Dirt doesn't just exist passively in the kitchen; it is personified: It "triumphs," "crawls," and lives "in delirious communion with the corrupted walls." The rug in the parlor, once beautiful, is now frayed from use and impossibly dirty, demons adding dirt while John tries to remove it. Even the family and neighborhood church is a storefront—a used, converted (from its original intended purpose), and dust laden environment.

Religion for this community is not merely a Sunday, once-a-week happening; it is a part of everyday life. Because there appears to be no avenue of escape from one's oppression in this world, one holds out hope it will happen in the next. Consequently, religion and religious activities are of primary importance. Because of this, Baldwin uses numerous religious and biblical references, allusions, and parallels to communicate and emphasize his themes. (The reader will do well to keep a copy of the Bible with a decent concordance close at hand.) Following are some of the more important allusions.

The phrase "Go tell it on the Mountain" is, itself, a verse from an African-American spiritual: "Go, tell it on the Mountain, over the hills and everywhere, that Jesus Christ is born!"

Character Insight

Many of the characters have biblical names that reflect their personalities, mirror their biblical counterparts, or add depth or subtle meaning to their character. Gabriel, for example (see the Character Analyses for further identification), is an angel in the Bible who acts as God's messenger. The name itself means "mighty man of God." As a minister, the character Gabriel in the novel does indeed bring the word of God to his neighbors, and he is mighty in the lives of his family members. Also, the biblical Elizabeth is a very devout woman who was a cousin to the Virgin Mary. God promised and gave the barren Elizabeth a son in her old age. Her son was John the Baptist. Baldwin's Elizabeth is the mother of John, the central character. (There is some scholarly debate over which John in the Bible John Grimes is intended to mirror. Some argue that he is intended to be John the Baptist whose mother was Elizabeth. John baptized the holy, including his cousin, Jesus, while prophesizing that God himself would later baptize them with the Holy Spirit and with fire. Other scholars insist that it is John of Patmos whom John Grimes is intended to resemble. They argue that there are many correlations between this biblical John and the novel's John, including several passages that are closely paralleled. Also, Baldwin's John is helped through his struggle on the threshing floor by recalling a religious song about John of Patmos.)

Character Insight

The biblical Deborah, the name in the novel of Gabriel's first wife, is a prophet and the only female Judge in the Bible who, with exemplary faith and courage, assisted in defeating the Canaanites and saving Israel, *circa* 1200 b.c. Elisha, whose name means "God is salvation," was a miracle worker of the Old Testament and, therefore, preceded Jesus. Although he was available to all social strata, Elisha ministered mainly among the common and poor people. He was very sensitive to the needs of the suffering and performed miracles to alleviate their pain. The novel's Elisha is much like his namesake. While he does not raise the dead or multiply food, he is still very close to his

Lord and often overcome by spiritual ecstasy, falling down and speaking in tongues. He preaches salvation to the young John and acts as his friend while the boy is going through a difficult period in his life. He lessens John's mental anguish and the pain of his solitude.

Finally, the scriptural tone and syntax of the language Baldwin uses throughout the novel demonstrates biblical influence in the everyday lives and language of the community.

In the short, opening paragraph of the novel, Baldwin introduces several conflicts and issues in the life of one of the central characters of the novel, John Grimes. These various issues include John's conflict with religion in general and the ministry specifically (as evidenced in the narrator's observations that "Everyone had always said he would be a preacher just like his father . . . ;" "John, without ever really thinking about, had come to believe it;" and by the age of 14, ". . . it was already too late" to change this fate); the conflict between John and his father; the conflict with his society (as represented by the "everyones" in this paragraph and their collective expectation that he would become a preacher); and the conflicts associated with pubescence (he is just turning 14).

But more significantly, a few pages later, the careful reader is already sensing that there is another—perhaps, more serious—conflict present: Something is wrong in this community of individuals who demonstrate or articulate personal feelings of frustration, of helplessness, and of dissatisfaction because of their inability to control or to have significant influence over their lives and circumstances—a far cry from having dominion over all other things. In addition, there is much more here than the typical conflicts faced by just any young male facing manhood, even one who is also wrestling with his religious identity and beliefs.

Through John, his family, and his environment, Baldwin exposes the social and psychological devolution of a people who have suffered and continue to suffer the insidious affects of racism from which there appears to be no escape, save death. The characters in the novel are only slightly removed (a generation or two) from their slave ancestors. We learn, for example, in Part Two, that Gabriel and Florence's mother was a slave, freed only by the Emancipation Proclamation and the Civil War. The novel takes place in 1935, only 73 years after the signing of the Emancipation Proclamation (1862) and 70 years after Robert E. Lee surrendered to Ulysses S. Grant (April 1865), ending the American Civil War, and the ratification of the 13th Amendment abolishing slavery (December 1865).

As a result of this proximity to slavery, the characters of the novel suffer a special set of physical, psychological, and social circumstances: As we learn later, Gabriel and Florence, for example, have siblings they will never know because, as property, their siblings were taken from their mother for various reasons (but all having to do with their slave—therefore, race—status and circumstances); the Great Migration (the journey north for many southern blacks) originally held promise of better times and circumstances for each character but ultimately resulted in only a different, often more oppressive, manifestation of the racism they were attempting to escape.

These outcomes and consequences of the American slave era and other vestiges of this period constitute the racism that Baldwin depicts in *Go Tell It on the Mountain*: It is second and third generation, slave-psyche racism, a racism based on the notion that one group of people is socially, genetically, and intentionally superior to another. This form of racism works its evil and malice on both the perpetrator and the victim.

Our very nature and culture cause us to defend what we do as morally right or definitely not wrong or, at least, morally neutral. Here and there, evil individuals may deliberately do evil things, but most of us feel a need to convince ourselves—and, most often, others—that what we do is, at least, not wrong. Therefore, we construct a rationale that justifies our actions. And so it was with the justification of slavery and racial categorizing. In subsequent generations, these rationales are accepted as moral or ethical truths. Hence, at some point, one or both populations may generally believe and endorse religious fabrications, such as the African-American blackness being the mark of Ham (Genesis IX, 25); distorted cultural values, such as lighter skin tones are "better" than darker skin tones; diminished expectations or standards of success and satisfaction, such as, a "storefront church" or merely "putting food on the table" or "clothes on the back" as being sufficient; or they may resort to opiates for escape, such as drinking and exaggerated adherence to religion and religious activity.

Theme

Baldwin demonstrates this affect of racism in each of his major characters, but in the two main characters, John and Gabriel—father and son—most vividly. John is the central character in the story's main plot (the maturation of a boy physically and religiously) while Gabriel figures most prominently in its major theme (the tragic effects of racism on a people and a society). Each character is the product of his environment, and each reflects the debilitating nature and consequences of the racism in his environment.

The plot of the story concentrates on the man-child, John, who is just turning 14 and wrestling both with the natural biological transformation that is taking place within him and with his confused social and religious status. John sees himself connected to evil. In part, he feels this because Gabriel, the second most significant character in the plot, has told him seriously and often that he is ugly and that the face of Satan can be seen in his features. But John also feels this way, in part, because he is reacting as a normal young male reacts who, during puberty, is confused by the irresistible urges of his new sexuality juxtaposed to the social, religious, and parental proscriptions against them.

Baldwin emphasizes John's sexual-moral conflict in the incident on the morning of his birthday. While looking at a stain on the ceiling which in John's mind has begun to resemble a naked woman, his thoughts turn to his "sin" of masturbating in the restroom of his school while thinking of the older boys who competed to see "whose urine could arch higher" and he "had watched in himself a transformation of which he could never speak." Although these feelings and, in fact, these episodes fall well within what is normal for the pubescent male, John is not aware of that, and he believes that he is evil, that his "heart was hardened against the Lord."

Character Insight

We learn a good deal about John in this first part through the literary device of character foil. The reader is informed of the differences between John and his younger brother, Roy: John is the good son, and Roy has a reputation as the typical bad seed. Whereas John is expected to become a minister, Roy looks as if he is headed for damnation. Roy is unabashed and boastful about his sexual conquests involving some of the girls in the neighborhood, and he frequently watches the prostitutes in the basement of a condemned house, which John avoids doing. John's virtues are reflected by Roy's apparent vices.

This relationship is often troublesome for John because he is expected to act as a good example to his younger brother and is often reprimanded for Roy's actions. John is held to a higher standard by his parents and everyone else in the community and is chastised for slight deviations while Roy trespasses with impunity because it is his expected behavior. For example, when neither John nor Roy know the Sunday school lessons, John's forgetfulness "earned him the wrath of his father," but "no one really expected of Roy what was expected of John." Also, unless Gabriel keeps a strict eye on Roy, Roy would disappear after Sunday school and not return to morning service. He would, in fact, be gone all day. It is in this manner that Baldwin reveals to the reader John's character. We find out who John *is* through direct description, and we find out who John is *not* through descriptions of Roy.

Baldwin further develops John's conflicts with his father and his religion in the episode of the movie house in the city. The city acts as an unholy lure for John. On Broadway, John sees beautiful lights and magnificent towers, movie theaters, and motor cars. Here John imagines being rich and loved. It is a lure that is more attractive than the alternative: his own surroundings, the buildings, "huddled, flat, ignoble, close to the filthy ground, where the streets and the hallways, and the rooms were dark, and where the unconquerable odor was of dust, and sweat, and urine, and homemade gin." John has "seen rich people in fancy clothes but never an angel of the lord robed in white. He has looked upon all sorts of finery in the shop windows but has never had a glimpse of the kingdom of heaven. He sees that the way of the cross had given [Gabriel] a belly filled with wind and bent his mother's back," but John has never seen religion make anyone happy or strong. How can one doubt that a child of barely 14 would be tempted by the broad way to shun the narrow way? The rewards which he had been promised in heaven for a good and holy life "were unimaginable—but the city was real."

One real pleasure of the city for John is the movie houses, movie houses forbidden by Gabriel. So, ignoring Gabriel's mandate against them, John quickly enters the theater lest he be seen by a member of his church, revealing that John, too, feels guilt about attending the movie, guilt beyond his father's admonishments. John initially chooses this particular movie because he identifies with the young man on the advertisement. However, by the end of the film, John wants to be like the cruel woman who torments the main character. She is proud and strong and able to tell the whole world, "You can kiss my ass." John sees these as desirable characteristics because he has constant feelings of humility and contrition. He lacks the strength to stand up against his father or his community to protect himself. John, who is forever holding back, not expressing all that he desires, wants the freedom of expression that this wicked, godless woman has. In the end, the woman dies and John imagines that her soul is transported to hell, which makes him think twice about his plans to emulate her. He believes that God led him to this movie to reinforce the teachings of his church. Thus, John's dilemma is defined: the narrow way (the church) or the broad way (the material world).

The character with the most thematic significance is Gabriel, who has a major impact on every other character's life. Gabriel is the product of the racist environments in which he has existed from birth. He has suffered the anxiety and confusion of the Southern, newly freed, slave environment; the anticipation and separation anxieties associated with the Great Migration; and the angst and ego-devastating environment of the Northern oppression and bigotry. In Part One, we learn that Gabriel is viewed differently by different characters.

The theme that permeates the novel and that Gabriel's character in particular illustrates is that of racism and its various forms and consequences. Racism is evident in nearly every paragraph of the work. Every character, in large part, is the result and product of racist concepts, racist values, and racist activities. The views of John and Gabriel regarding racism are polar opposites. But John is yet a child, naïve and inexperienced; Gabriel has suffered the realities of his subordinate position in a racist society; he is embittered, hardened, and defeated. While John recalls the kindness of a concerned teacher when he was sick, Gabriel can think only of injustices that African Americans endured where he grew up and where he lives.

John is not without racist attitudes, however. John, in fact, illustrates the most tragic and insidious variety of racism, racism directed against one's own people and hence oneself. While disparaging the compliments of those of his own race, John revels in the fact that he has also been singled out for praise by whites. Baldwin writes: "John was not much interested in his people . . ." and "It was not only colored people who praised John, since they could not, John felt, in any case really know." When his white school principal tells John that he is a "very bright boy," John sees a new life opening up, but when his neighbors tell him that he will be a great leader of his people, he is unmoved.

Because John has had no overt, negative experiences with whites, "it was hard for him to think of them burning in hell forever," as Gabriel promises they will. Gabriel proclaims whites to be wicked and untrustworthy, warning John that, when he is older, he will find out for himself how evil they really are. John has read about racism and the injustices and tortures that blacks had endured in the South, but he has experienced none of these things himself. He recalls a white teacher who brought him medicine when he was ill. He knows that there are regulations that prohibit him from living side by side with whites in the fancy apartment building that he passes, but no one has accosted him during his walk. Quite the opposite, when he ran down the hill in Central Park, he nearly knocked down an old white man. Surprised, but far from being angry, the man smiled at John, who smiled back. It was nothing but kindness and pure affection for a stranger, another human being, which passed between the two in that smile.

Character Insight

Oppression is always about power of some sort, and the power in *Mountain* appears to be heavily skewed in Gabriel's favor. He wants it all, and, in relation to his family, he has it all. If family members disagree with him or do something he does not like, he physically attacks them. In the larger context, however, in issues relating to having dominion, sovereignty, or control over one's life, Gabriel has been emasculated. Gabriel's dominance of family is an illustration of a diminished and distorted standard of power. The reader learns that, at one time, Gabriel was very powerful in the community also. When he was still living in the South, his name was known far and wide, and he was considered a great man of God. He traveled widely, his name appearing on great signs that heralded his arrival. It was after he moved north and had a family to provide for that his status, and hence his power, decreased. Instead of caring for the flock's souls, he was relegated to changing their light bulbs. It may be partially due to his loss of status in the community that Gabriel rules his family with an iron fist. Overcompensation at home does not replace his lost glory, but it helps to ease the blow.

John is also developing a sense that he, too, is powerful. When the school principal tells him that he is bright, he sees not only power but also salvation. He immediately grasps that his intelligence is power, a power, he feels, that will assist him in escaping his oppression which, at this point in his maturation, he sees as his dominant father. Someday John will be able to raise himself out of his father's world, which he does not want for himself. It is John's conflict with his father that feeds his intellect. Although John sees himself as having a heart full of sin for rejecting his father's life, he understands that his head will lead him to a different life.

Literary Device

A common literary device used by Baldwin in this section is that of foreshadowing, which predicts something in the future that the character (and sometimes the reader) knows nothing about. Perhaps the line most full of foreshadowing because it calls upon two separate events is spoken by Elizabeth. During her argument with Roy, she warns him against his headstrong ways, saying that it appears that he won't stop "till someone puts a knife in you." Later that same day, someone does indeed put a knife into Roy. Elizabeth's line also conjures up another event. Royal, Gabriel's unclaimed son, died from a stab wound he received over a game of cards.

The actual stabbing of Roy again calls to mind Royal's death. Elizabeth inadvertently calls up Royal's death when she suggests to Gabriel that they pray to God to stop Roy before he receives a mortal wound. Her unwitting reminder to Gabriel of his first son earns her a blow that knocks her to the floor. Despite the fact that Roy's wound is to his forehead, Gabriel says that his attackers were trying to cut his throat. Again, it was Royal whose wound was to the throat. That Royal's death is referenced four separate times in such a short period suggests its significance.

Glossary

tarry   to wait: in this context, to wait for the Lord.

Tarry Service   Saturday evening service in which the churchgoers wait for the Lord to speak to them.

saints   members of the Church of the Fire Baptized who have been saved.

deadlock   a tie between opponents in the course of a contest.

Harlot   a prostitute.

blasphemous   irreverent or profane.

golden text   Holy scripture; the Bible.

squalling   crying or screaming loudly and harshly.

Redeemer   here, God.

malevolent   having or showing ill will; malicious.

ravenous   greedily or wildly hungry; voracious or famished.

commune   to talk together intimately.

testify   to bear witness to; affirm; declare.

the Word   here, the word of God; Holy Scripture.

Part Two: The Prayers of the Saints
One: Florence's Prayer

Summary

Kneeling before the altar, Florence recalls her mother and remembers that it was she who first taught her how to pray, how to humble herself before the Lord. Now, however, Florence feels more bitter than humble because she knows that she is dying. She remembers all the people who influenced her life, for better or worse, and wants their forgiveness for injustices she believes she perpetrated against them.

Florence looks back on her life, beginning with a night when she was 13, huddled in the small cabin that she shared with her mother and her brother, Gabriel. They feared that their home would be burned down by white men in a way of retaliation for a father's threat of retribution for the gang rape of his daughter Deborah. The horses and riders passed, and they knew themselves to be safe for the time being.

Florence's mother, Rachel, had been a slave before she was freed by the Civil War and had suffered all the miseries and injustices of her position. She had lost several children through death or auction; she had even had one, whom she was never allowed to see, taken away to live in the master's house. For these reasons, Gabriel and Florence were especially precious to her. However, being a boy in a male-centered society, Gabriel was even more special to her.

Gabriel had been their mother's favorite since his birth, and Florence feels cheated of the things that she wanted but that were given to Gabriel instead. He had a chance to attend school, he had the best clothes and food that the family was able to afford, and he had the care of his mother and sister. Yet Gabriel never appreciated what he was given and carelessly squandered it all. When Gabriel was young, he made mischief around town. As he grew older, he took to drinking and loose women, coming home blind drunk and covered with his own vomit.

When Florence was 26, after her employer made an improper sexual advance toward her, Florence bought a ticket to New York City, packed a bag, and left home. She left behind her dying mother, her drunken and bewildered brother, and her good friend Deborah.

In New York, Florence married a man named Frank. Their marriage lasted for more than 10 years before he left her after an especially bitter argument. Rather than being depressed over this turn of circumstances, however, Florence was relieved. Frank moved in with another woman and later died overseas during WWI. Florence thinks now that she would like to find Frank's grave and place flowers on it, and she wonders how he died.

Florence weeps for the lost Frank and hears Gabriel's voice behind her. The sound of his voice triggers thoughts of her friend and his first wife, Deborah. Once, Florence had received a letter from Deborah telling of Deborah's suspicions that Gabriel had fathered a son by another woman. For years, Florence had planned to show that letter to Gabriel; even tonight, at the church service, the letter is in her purse. Now she wonders whether Deborah had ever confronted Gabriel with her suspicions, and she wonders if she will ever show him the letter that she has carried for over 20 years. Florence has been waiting for a time when revealing the letter could do the most damage to her brother. She realizes that she will probably be dead before the long awaited day when her evidence could bring about his destruction.

Florence is suddenly furious at God for loving her mother and brother more than loving her. She is angry that she, "who had only sought to walk upright," was to die while her brother, who wallowed in sin, was allowed to live. And she is angry that her mother in heaven will see her daughter's descent into hell. Florence collapses sobbing at the altar and feels the hand of death upon her and hears its voice warn her that her time to die is approaching.

Commentary

After the incident in which Florence sees death by her bedside, she is haunted by thoughts of people from her past and how she has betrayed and hurt them. To the reader, this remorse is unwarranted. Florence is, or at least at one time had been, a strong-willed, independent woman and one of the most blameless characters in the novel.

Her desertion of her mother came only after her employer's sexual advances, when she realized that her time in that place had come to its inevitable end. Her moving north and leaving her family had nothing to do with having a cold heart. She simply wanted something better for herself than she believed she could find where she was. She didn't want to exchange her mother's cabin for one of her own and work herself to death as her mother had. Besides, Gabriel was still at home, and it seems only fair that he would have to return to his mother some of the care that she had lavished upon him for so many years.

Florence's guilt concerning Gabriel also seems out of place. That she "held him to scorn and mocked his ministry" is, to some degree, justified. No one knows Gabriel better than Florence does. She has seen Gabriel at his very worst and is not impressed by his best. She sees him as a liar, a hypocrite, and even as a murderer for letting the mother of his baby run off to die alone in childbirth. In short, according to Florence, Gabriel is not fit for the ministry.

Why the ghost of Deborah should come to haunt the only friend she ever had is a mystery. Their friendship lasted long after Florence left home. It was Florence to whom Deborah wrote when Deborah needed council. The letter that Florence carries in her purse testifies to that fact. Deborah trusted Florence enough to speak of her horrible fear. That only Florence knows the truth indicates that, obviously, Deborah felt that she could trust this secret to anyone else. Florence's feelings of guilt concerning Frank are the most understandable. Frank left after 10 years of bitter fighting, disappointments, and misplaced efforts on both sides. However, that Florence shoulders *all* the blame for a failed marriage is unrealistic and unfair. Florence's desire to place flowers on his grave in France so many years after their break is proof that there was affection and tender feelings in her relationship with Frank.

Theme

As the title of the novel suggests, each of the characters has an obstacle or mountain to overcome to reach his or her own salvation. Florence's mountain arises from her feelings of powerlessness. All the advantages that her mother could afford were given to Gabriel, and Florence could only watch helplessly as he squandered those gifts that she so desired but was unable to acquire for herself. In a desperate attempt to empower herself, she left her mother and brother and struck out on her own to New York City where she believed that she could find better opportunities and advantages. Once in New York, Florence married Frank because she believed that she could change him. At her insistence, he was willing to do small things such as shave, change his clothes, and go to "Uplift meetings," where speakers talked about the "future and duties of the Negro race." Yet Florence's marriage failed when she realized that she had no power to change Frank's personality and that she could not transform him into the man whom she truly desired.

Her coming death is another way Florence's powerlessness manifests itself. Her own body has betrayed her by becoming filled with an unnamed sickness for which she is powerless to find a cure. Despite the hope that she invested in her female acquaintances, doctors, and herbal teas and powders, her pain becomes stronger while her body becomes weaker.

Florence carries in her purse a letter that she hopes will give her power over Gabriel. The fact that she has never used the letter to her advantage hints that she fears that this proof of his infidelity will be ineffective against her brother, who has for so long been such a powerful force in her life and in the lives of others. No one but Florence knows of the existence of the letter, and she has never revealed its contents to anyone—not even Elizabeth, who was her friend before Elizabeth's marriage to Gabriel and who could have been saved from a marriage built on lies and full of brutality if she had realized the true nature of the man she chose to marry. Even Elizabeth's son John could have been saved from a life of heartache and rejection. Florence has not taken the advice she gave to Deborah so long ago to confront Gabriel with the truth. Now she sees that her opportunity to gain power over her brother is almost lost.

Character Insight

The irony of this situation is that Florence is the *only* character with any power over Gabriel. Even their mother, with all her beatings, could not control the young Gabriel. Recall the scene at John's house after Roy has been stabbed. Florence argues with and stands up to Gabriel with impunity; Gabriel simply tells her to shut up. But when Elizabeth speaks her mind to Gabriel, he strikes her. When Gabriel beats Roy, it is Florence who stops him by grabbing the belt. Her words to her brother after that awful scene mirror her own world view, "You can't change nothing, Gabriel. You ought to know that by now."

Florence is unable to see her own strength, not only in her relationship with her brother, but with others in her life as well. Her friendship with Deborah undoubtedly gave Deborah comfort and succor after the trauma of her rape. A weak woman would not have been able to leave friends and family behind and move hundreds of miles away in the year 1900. Florence was able to support herself after being abandoned by her husband, and she provided not only friendship but also strength and support to the unwed Elizabeth. Her real weakness comes from not being aware of her own power and accomplishments.

Theme

The desire for freedom plays an important role in the novel. The reader learns very early in Florence's story that her mother had been a slave. The story that the old woman tells of her emancipation from slavery is the only tale that held any meaning for the young Florence. Her mother's departure from her place of bondage was a story that Florence would never forget, and it became her own dream "to walk out one morning through the cabin door, never to return." While Rachel's freedom was from the bondage of slavery, Florence's was from her home, which held no future for her except that of unrewarding toil and thankless labor. And she departed, just as her father had done so many years ago, to the promised land of the North. Despite her mother's protests, Florence "knew that her mother had understood, had indeed long before this moment known that this time would come."

Literary Device

The allusions of Bathsheba (Rachel's friend who brought the news of freedom) and Rachel to Egypt and the plagues give their own plight greater meaning and tie them to ancient suffering. The slaves identified themselves with the Israelites who were also slaves in a foreign land. Because God delivered the Israelites into freedom as he had promised, the American slaves felt the assurance that God would deliver them from bondage one day, as well. By incorporating these biblical allusions into their plight, Baldwin makes their story more universal and, probably, more tolerable.

Finally, we see the impact of systemic racism on Florence in her aversion to blackness; she uses skin whiteners (symbolic of self hatred) for Frank's pleasure, but Frank tells her, "black's a mighty pretty color." She dislikes "common niggers," a symptom of a racist cataloguing within the race. Without knowing how or when, Florence has bought the racist lie.

Glossary

abdicate   to give up formally (a high office, throne, authority, etc.).

Hezekiah   a biblical king of Judah in the time of Isaiah: 2 Kings 18–20.

forsaken   abandoned; desolate; forlorn.

armies had come from the North to set them free   reference to Union forces that fought in the South during the U.S. Civil War and, as they traveled between battles, freed southern slaves.

Slaves done ris "Slaves have risen," a reference to a slave revolt at another plantation in which one or more slaves had turned against an oppressor.

judgment trumpet one of seven trumpets that will herald the apocalypse.

plagues with which the lord had afflicted Egypt reference to the ten plagues that God sent to Egypt so that the Israelites would be released from slavery and allowed to leave.

He done brought us out of Egypt God has set them free from slavery; a biblical allusion to the Israelites being led out of Egypt and slavery.

switch a thin flexible twig or stick used for whipping.

Peter and Paul in the dungeon cell reference to two Christian apostles who were martyred, probably during the reign of Nero.

the war WWI.

bleaching cream a lotion used to lighten the skin.

Part Two: The Prayers of the Saints
Two: Gabriel's Prayer

Summary

Florence's cry meets Gabriel's ears not as his sisters voice, but as the voice of any number of sinners, including his own, when crying out for God's mercy. In the silence following her cry, Gabriel is transported back to the days before he was saved.

Gabriel's mother refused to die until she saw the last of her children saved. Sometimes, Deborah would sit with Gabriel's mother, and she and his mother would watch in silence as Gabriel got ready to go out drinking. He felt guilty about what he was doing, but did it nonetheless.

Coming home from a night spent with a woman from out of town and having drunk too much whiskey, Gabriel felt that all the world stood still to look at his sins and see him cast away from God. He fell against a nearby tree, calling for mercy, but felt that he had sinned for too long and that God had turned away from him. Suddenly, he heard his mother singing for him. He praised God, turned from sin, and felt himself reborn.

Gabriel began to preach, and Deborah began to look after him following his mother's death. She cooked his meals, did his laundry, and encouraged him with her praise of his sermons. Deborah had no husband nor even any suitors. The memory of her rape was a barrier between her and the community. She was perfectly suited to take care of the sick and dying, but no respectable man would dream of making her his wife. Still, she was a pillar of strength for Gabriel by helping him through his new life and vocation as minister.

Gabriel was asked that summer to preach at the Twenty-Four Elders Revival Meeting. There he would preach with distinguished ministers. Gabriel was honored and nervous about his performance, and he and Deborah prayed and fasted before he was to speak. On the appointed night, Gabriel and Deborah went together to the revival, and Gabriel asked Deborah to sit where he could see her. He mounted the pulpit, asked Deborah to read a passage from the Bible for him, and then began his sermon—a lecture on sin and salvation and the mercy of Jesus. At the conclusion of Gabriel's sermon, a young man knelt on the altar weeping, seeking forgiveness. Gabriel felt that the Lord had spoken through him, and he saw that the elders approved of his sermon.

The Sunday of the great dinner came, and Gabriel was uncomfortable around these men of faith. He found them too worldly and too well fed. He discovered that they all had a repertoire of sermons that no longer really came from their hearts and so felt that they were not giving God his full due. Deborah served the ministers that night, and after her departure from the room, one of the elders joked about her rape. Enraged, Gabriel rebuked the ministers for their laughter. Gabriel believed that the others were shamed by his purity, and he saw himself sitting by the right hand of God. Suddenly, he questioned God's plan concerning his relationship with Deborah. Perhaps it was God's will that the two of them should wed. Because Deborah helped him to stand as a man, now he could erase her shame and raise her to a place of honor as a woman. No longer would she be the girl who was raped, the girl looked at with a mixture of lust and repugnance; instead, she would be the esteemed wife of Reverend Grimes. Through her, Gabriel thought, he would sire his line of holy children. He decided to pray and to ask the Lord's will.

That night while walking her home, Gabriel asked Deborah to pray to help him to discover God's will over a matter that God had placed upon Gabriel's heart. Later that night, Gabriel had two dreams, which he interpreted to mean that God did intend for Gabriel to marry Deborah. Gabriel proposed the next day, and Deborah accepted.

Cries from Elisha, who is overcome by God's power, interrupt Gabriel's reverie. For a moment, Gabriel fears that the cries come from John. Then he becomes angry that his own sons are not present and have never been saved. One son (Royal) is long dead, and the other (Roy) is at home, wounded and angry with his father. Because Royal was a bastard, Gabriel thinks, it is understandable that he should be lost to sin, but his second son, Roy, was conceived in marriage and, therefore, should be saved. Gabriel is sure that Roy is not being punished for Gabriel's sins, so he concludes that Roy is being punished because of sins for which Roy's mother, Elizabeth, has not fully repented.

After Gabriel's marriage to Elizabeth, Elizabeth insisted that they not treat John differently than any of their other children, but Gabriel believes that there is a difference between John, a child who is not biologically his, and the children he sired. In Gabriel's eyes, John is the child of a "weak, proud woman and some careless boy," while Roy is the son God had promised Gabriel to carry on his name and to do the Lord's work. Gabriel has repented the death of Ester, the mother of his first son (Royal), and the death of Royal himself as a young man.

Ester moved into town soon after Gabriel's marriage to Deborah and worked for the same family that Gabriel worked for. She had many boyfriends and, like her mother and stepfather, rarely went to church. One afternoon, Gabriel invited Ester to hear him preach. Ester arrived at the church with her mother. After preaching a sermon that was remembered for years to come, Gabriel called for sinners to come forth and be saved. When Ester did not rise, Gabriel was filled with rage. Not long afterwards, Gabriel and Ester had an affair that lasted for only nine days before Gabriel ended it. By this time, however, Ester was pregnant.

When Ester told him of her pregnancy, Gabriel questioned whether they baby was, indeed, his. Offended, Ester insisted that she had not been with so many men that she could be confused about the child's parentage. Then she suggested that the two of them run away. When Gabriel refused, Ester demanded money to go away by herself and threatened to tell that Gabriel was the father of her unborn baby if he refused her the money. That night, Gabriel stole money that Deborah had been saving and gave it to Ester. A week later, Ester left for Chicago, telling her parents that she was looking for a better life.

On the road again preaching, Gabriel did not find the peace he sought; in fact, he found just the opposite. He saw the suffering of others much more clearly and saw how far they had strayed from the word of God. He began to pray for Ester, and although he saw the bleakness in the lives of others, he found in himself a new faith and vowed never to wander into a life of sin again.

Ester died in childbirth, and Ester's mother brought her daughter's body and her grandson home. Gabriel and Deborah attended Ester's funeral, where Ester's stepfather held Gabriel's son, Royal. Still Gabriel did not claim the child. Deborah became more friendly with Ester's family and reported how the boy was loved and spoiled by his grandparents. Gabriel watched his son grow up and into the life of sin that Ester had led. Gabriel found that whenever Deborah spoke of Royal, he was afraid that she knew the truth, and he had often thought to confess and unburden his heart. He wanted to tell her that he was Royal's father and that he hated Deborah for her inability to have children.

Royal left town but returned inauspiciously soon after a black soldier had been found lynched just outside of town. Gabriel ran into

Royal on the street that night and warned him of the danger of being out at that hour and advised Royal to find his way home. Royal, however, didn't share Gabriel's fear because, he said, the white's appetite for blood had been satisfied.

Back in the present, John tries to pray. He contemplates salvation and wonders why, if God can heal all troubles, his parents, who have been saved, are not happy. John waits for the time when God will reach down and raise him up, the time when he will no longer be Gabriel's son, but instead be a son of his Heavenly Father. When this happens, John thinks that Gabriel will be forced to treat him fairly and to love him. Strangely enough, John realizes that Gabriel's love is not what John really wants. He wants to be justified in his hatred of his father and is not willing now to trade in so many years of abuse for love. He wishes his father were dead so that he could laugh at his screams in hell.

Gabriel remembers the stormy day that Deborah told him that Royal had been killed in a barroom in Chicago. During this conversation, Deborah finally asked Gabriel if Royal was his son, and Gabriel admitted the truth. He was openly angry with Deborah for her inability to bear him a son, and she said that if he had confessed at Ester's funeral, she would have raised the dead woman's son as her own. She advises Gabriel to pray for forgiveness.

Back in the present, Gabriel stands over Elisha, who is lying on the floor. Gabriel remembers his marriage to Elizabeth, an event that he believed was a sign that God had forgiven him. He looks at his wife's son, John, who returns his stare. Gabriel believes it is the Devil who looks out of the boy's eyes and would have struck him if Elisha, who is now speaking in tongues, were not between the two.

Commentary

Character Insight

Gabriel does not accept blame or take responsibility for his actions. He blames Ester for their affair, asserting that she tempted him. Ester believes that it was he who instigated the relationship. She later tells him, "That weren't no reverend looking at me them mornings in the yard." Remember that Gabriel reached out to Ester first that night in the kitchen and that Ester protested that they not have sex on the kitchen floor of their employer's home. Even after Ester tells him of her pregnancy, Gabriel denies the possibility that the child can be his. When Ester finally convinces him that the child is indeed his and asks what they should do, Gabriel councils her to "get one of these boys you been running around with to marry you. Because I can't go off with you nowhere." Only after she threatens to expose their affair to the townspeople does Gabriel agree to help her. He steals money from his wife, not to help his mistress, but to save his own reputation.

After the death of Ester and her son, Gabriel blames both tragedies on Deborah, implying that both could have been prevented if it were not for their marriage and his obligation to her. Even his refusal to claim his own motherless child he blames on Deborah, claiming that she never gave him an opportunity to tell the truth, a claim that is blatantly untrue. Deborah gave Gabriel the chance when she speculated about the father's identity and commented how much Royal reminded her of Gabriel at the same age. Deborah knew the truth, but she was waiting to hear it from Gabriel.

Here Gabriel distorts history to suit his own needs. He never intended to run off with Ester. Even had he not been married at the time of the affair, he still would not have made Ester his wife. Nor would he have accepted Royal as his son. Had he taken on the responsibility of raising his son, people would then have known that he, their reverend, had sinned, and he was unwilling to lose the esteem of his flock. Implying that he would have married the girl if not for his marriage to Deborah or that he would have claimed his son if he had only been given the opportunity are his ways of shifting responsibility away from himself and on to the shoulders of someone else, in this case to Deborah.

Gabriel blames Elizabeth for Roy's stabbing, implying that she is a bad mother because she cannot control the rebellious boy. He says that his own mother would have found a way to keep the child out of harm's way. Florence counters that even their mother could not stop Gabriel's wild ways and only "wore herself beating on you, just like you been wearing yourself out beating on this boy here." Gabriel cannot deny the truth in his sister's statement, but neither can he look at his own ways to find a solution to the problem. It does not occur to him that perhaps it is because he is a poor role model or that his parenting leaves much to be desired. He is a provider but not a real *father*, although the two terms are synonymous to him.

Character Insight

Gabriel hides behind his religious conversion and uses it to deflect responsibility. When people question his actions, he hides behind his Bible and position as preacher. His attitude, akin to "God has forgiven me so I don't need to answer to anyone else," shields him from feelings of guilt. The obstacle Gabriel must overcome to find salvation (his personal mountain, so to speak) is his struggle with sin, which manifests itself in arrogance. His very insistence on his personal innocence leads the reader to believe that unconsciously he is not so comfortable with the status of his soul. He repeats over and over that God has forgiven him, but he does not appear to have forgiven himself. Ester's words to Gabriel shortly before they have intercourse for the first time foreshadow Gabriel's predicament throughout the rest of the novel. She teased, "But I can't help it if you done things that *you's* ashamed of, Reverend."

People who have come to terms with past mistakes do not feel the need to make excuses for their actions the way that Gabriel does. Deborah sees that Gabriel is tormented by guilt the day that she tells him of Royal's death. When Gabriel argues that he could not have helped Ester because she would have led him to hell, Deborah counters that the dead woman "mighty near has." She knows that, if Gabriel does not find forgiveness, he will be forever in his own hell of guilt.

Gabriel believes that his marriage to Elizabeth is a sign that God has forgiven him, but it is obvious that he is still not comfortable with his past. If he were not still ashamed about his actions, he would have told Elizabeth about his first son. He has not. His guilt manifests itself in fury after Roy is stabbed. Elizabeth says that they should pray for God to change Roy's heart before he is stabbed again. Her unwitting allusion to the death of Gabriel's first son provokes such an avalanche of guilt that Gabriel strikes out at her. He cannot change the past, but he can punish anyone who reminds him of it.

Gabriel wants to be sure that Elizabeth has repented for her sin of having had a child (John) out of wedlock. It is a mistake that they have both made, but only Gabriel knows this; Elizabeth does not. Gabriel asks Elizabeth again and again if she is sorry for her actions because to know that she has fully repented for her sin and found forgiveness would make it easier for him to forgive himself. However, Gabriel realizes that Elizabeth would do nothing differently if she were able to relive her time with Richard (her first love and John's biological father) and that she refuses to be sorry that Richard's child was born. It is only after this realization that Gabriel begins to treat Elizabeth and John so poorly. Gabriel hates John not because he is another man's child or for anything that John himself has done, but because John is a constant reminder of his own sin for which he cannot forgive himself. Gabriel believes, as Florence says at the end of the novel, that if he can make

Elizabeth and John pay enough for Elizabeth's sin, then Roy will not have to pay for Gabriel's.

Gabriel has, in the past, been able to overcome his shame about his actions. In the first dream he had before asking Deborah to be his wife, he revisited his past sinful life. In the next dream, he had to climb a steep mountain to reach heaven. That mountain was made of all his former sins piled one on top of the other, but Gabriel was able to overcome them. When he speaks of the sinful life he lived prior to his religious conversion, he is not proud of his actions, but he is able to talk about them. But the sin he committed after his conversion—his affair with Ester and the child that resulted from it—he cannot outwardly acknowledge. He has told no one of his link to Royal, and he admitted the truth to Deborah only when she confronted him.

Finally, the powerful image of the castrated African-American soldier in this section graphically illustrates the racism-in-America theme. Issues of sex and sexuality (usually taking the form of white fears and myths related to sex organs, interracial rape, and so on) have forever been linked to the issues of race in America, and they persist even into this new millennium.

Glossary

Testimony   public avowal, as of faith or of a religious experience.

Lord's Anointed   a person chosen and blessed by God.

the throne   God's throne; here a church altar.

the vow   a promise to give up sinful ways and live life according to biblical precepts.

revival meeting   a large church gathering often held during the summer, outside or in a tent, during which people publicly confess their sins and renew their faith.

mercy seat   a place before the pulpit where a person kneels and asks for God's forgiveness.

bondwoman   a woman bound to service without pay: a slave.

the war   WWI.

speaking in tongues   glossolalia, ecstatic utterance of usually unintelligible speechlike sounds, as in a religious assembly, viewed by some as a manifestation of deep religious experience.

Part Two: The Prayers of the Saints
Three: Elizabeth's Prayer

Summary

While Elisha is speaking in tongues, Elizabeth fears that God is speaking to her, condemning her for her sins and warning her of trials yet to come. When Elisha rises and seats himself at the piano, the song he plays reminds Elizabeth of her aunt and how Elizabeth had come to live in her aunt's house.

Elizabeth had never been close to her mother, who was very beautiful but frail. Her mother had not been affectionate with her, and Elizabeth attributed this lack of affection to the fact that Elizabeth was much darker and not as beautiful as her mother. Elizabeth was, however, quite close to her father whom she had loved dearly and with whom she had spent much time.

Following her mother's death, Elizabeth's maternal aunt took her away from her father, who ran a house of prostitution, declaring that he was unfit to raise a little girl. Elizabeth was devastated and hated her aunt. She screamed and cried at the railway station when she was taken from him and had to be carried to the train that would take her to her aunt's house.

Elizabeth knew that her aunt would never love her, even though the woman professed that she did. Her aunt prophesied that Elizabeth would fall from grace because of her pride, but it was only Elizabeth's pride and bitterness against her aunt that allowed her to endure her life in her aunt's house. These thoughts make Elizabeth think of Richard, the man who took her out of her aunt's house, the man whom she had loved more than she had loved God—and she believes it was for this reason that Richard was taken from her.

Richard worked at a local grocery. Elizabeth met him when she went into the store to buy some lemons. He smiled at her, and they spoke briefly and she left, but it was the beginning of their romance. Elizabeth fought for and won permission from her aunt to move to New York City (with Richard, unbeknownst to her aunt). Elizabeth told her aunt that she wanted to take advantage of the greater opportunities the North held.

In New York City, Elizabeth lived with a female relative and found work at the same hotel as Richard. The two planned to marry as soon as Richard saved some money, but, because he made so little and was also attending school, their wedding was not in the foreseeable future.

Despite her happiness with Richard, Elizabeth saw that there was little difference between the North and the South. The North promised but did not give, and what a person could take was snatched right back away again. Then one Sunday, Richard did not arrive for the dinner at which he was to meet the woman with whom Elizabeth was staying, and on Monday, he was not at work. Elizabeth shortly after discovered that Richard was a suspect in a robbery and had been arrested. She visited him in jail, and he told her what happened: The three young men who had robbed a store ran down into the subway and stood by Richard. When the police caught up with the three, the police assumed that Richard was with the robbers and arrested him too. The white store-owner identified the group as those who had robbed and stabbed him. Richard was beaten when he refused to sign a confession.

Elizabeth was terrified. She knew that she was pregnant and wondered what would happen if Richard was convicted and sent away. But Richard was found innocent of the charges and released. That night he wept in Elizabeth's arms, and she decided to wait to tell him that she was carrying his child. She never got the chance, however, because Richard committed suicide that night.

Back in the present, Elizabeth weeps for John, wondering what kind of trials he will have to face in his life. Would he be forced to pay for the sins of his mother and father? When he was born, should she have given him to another family who would have loved him more than her husband, Gabriel, ever had? She knows that if Gabriel loves her it is only because she is the mother of his son Roy. Then she remembers how she had come to know Gabriel.

Florence had been Elizabeth's friend. The two of them talked over coffee after work and talked about their lives. One Sunday, Elizabeth took the infant John to Florence's house. It was then that Florence told her that she had a brother who would be moving to New York soon. Though Florence had not seen Gabriel in more than 20 years, she was not looking forward to his arrival because she believed the years had not changed him.

Elizabeth met Gabriel a few weeks later, and he made her feel that there was hope that she could again be a woman worthy of respect.

Florence did not approve of the developing romance and often said so. Yet Gabriel was very good to Elizabeth and treated John as if he were his own son. When Gabriel asked Elizabeth to be his wife, promising to love and honor her and to provide for and love John like a son, she accepted his proposal.

A cry from John interrupts Elizabeth's reminiscence, and she opens her eyes to see John lying on the floor, overcome by the power of God.

Commentary

More so than any other character in the novel, Elizabeth represents love. Her children feel free to speak to her in a manner that they cannot communicate with their father. Roy says as much to her during their argument about Gabriel on the morning of John's birthday. He says, "[T]ell me how come he never let me talk to him like I talk to you?" Elizabeth is also the only person who remembers, or chooses to acknowledge, John's birthday. She is not able to give him much, but she gives him all that she can.

It is also significant that of all the marital and sexual relationships found in the novel, Elizabeth and Richard had the only alliance founded on love. Her marriage to Gabriel was based on hope that quickly disintegrated. Florence's marriage to Frank had affection and lust but nothing much deeper, and Gabriel's marriage to Deborah was more to spite the world than to love the woman. Although Deborah may have loved Gabriel—or at least respected him—the feeling was one sided. Richard loved Elizabeth just as much as she loved him, and their relationship was not built on lust or sex: They had been dating long before they began having intercourse. It is, perhaps, because of her love for Richard, that Elizabeth cherishes John as she does. He is all that she has left of the man whom she loved so desperately and the only reminder of the happy times she and Richard shared. Elizabeth's love for John is a natural continuation of her love for Richard. It should also be noted that Elizabeth is the only character the reader knows for certain to have had a healthy and loving relationship with her father. Gabriel's own father left shortly after his birth, just as Richard's had done. John never knew his biological father, and, as for the man he believes to be his father, he and his brother share a hatred for and a fear of him.

At first glance, Elizabeth and Florence seem to have little in common. The age difference between the two women alone would seem to be an insurmountable barrier. A closer look though reveals many similarities between the two women, but even their similarities belie their differences. The first and most obvious is the location of their birth. Both women are from the South, and both moved to New York City claiming a chance for better opportunities and looking to escape from unhappy homes. Florence had the strength and drive to leave by herself, while Elizabeth left on the arm of Richard.

The homes from which the two young women were running were headed by females who denied them what they most wanted. Florence's mother gave all the advantages that she was able to afford to the unthankful Gabriel, while Florence was helpless to claim any opportunities for herself. Elizabeth's aunt denied Elizabeth her father whom she loved to distraction. Even her own mother denied the young Elizabeth the love which is every child's right.

Both women were the strength in their respective relationship, but neither of them had any power. Florence failed in her attempt to control Frank (who also failed in his role as provider, never able to buy Florence the house or anything else which she really wanted). His attempts to compensate for this lack by buying her baubles and other useless knickknacks only served to infuriate his wife. For Richard, Elizabeth acted as a sort of emotional buoy. Even though their marriage was somewhere in the indefinite future and Elizabeth was not comfortable with Richard's godless ways, "She did not leave him, because, she was afraid of what might happen to him without her. She did not resist him, because he needed her." Still, in the end she was powerless to save him from false accusations and police brutality that brought about his suicide.

Finding themselves alone after the loss of their men, both women react in the same way. They lie. Florence claimed that Frank had died without having bought life insurance. Elizabeth bought and wore a wedding ring to disguise the real reason she has a child and no husband. If anyone questioned her, she explained that her husband had died. Elizabeth eventually told Florence the truth about her illegitimate son, but Florence never disclosed her own fabrication.

Florence and Elizabeth deal with their new-found status very differently. Florence remains single while Elizabeth marries as soon as an opportunity presents itself. Perhaps this different reaction can be explained by their very different experiences with relationships. Neither character has any reason to believe that a new relationship with a man would be any different from previous relationships. Of course, Florence would not want to enter into another union. Her experience with men has been less than perfect. Her father deserted her mother, she watched as the young Gabriel moved from woman to woman without a thought, and her own husband left her.

Elizabeth has had a very different experience with men. She has enjoyed happy and loving relationships with both her father and her lover. She believes that they were taken from her and that their separation is in no way the fault of the men. The loss of her father she blames on her aunt, and she shoulders the blame for the loss of Richard. She believes that if she had told him that she was carrying his child, "everything might have been very different, and he would be living yet." She also believes she loved Richard too much, and God took him from her for that very reason.

Despite their different experiences and choices, both women find themselves in very similar situations: beaten down and alone. Both have found that they are unprepared for the hardships that chance thrust upon them, and, by the end of their stories, we see that both women are overcome by their sorrows and ignorant of how to improve their situation. The reader sees also that they are both terribly disappointed and alone. Florence is alone in a literal sense. Unmarried and childless, she lives alone in a small apartment, and there is no mention of any friends. Elizabeth finds herself alone also despite the fact that she is surrounded by family. Gabriel is not someone in whom she can confide. He is physically and verbally abusive, someone more to be feared than loved. While she does care for her children, it is impossible to have a real friendship with one's very young child especially when the child is being brought up in a lie. It is also painfully obvious that none of the women in her church really know or understand her.

Furthermore, Elizabeth's friendship with Florence has been thwarted since Elizabeth's marriage to Gabriel because he acts as a barrier between the two women. There is a mutual trust, understanding, and respect between Florence and Elizabeth, but this is not allowed to grow because of the disrespect and distrust between Florence and Gabriel. Florence and Gabriel both hold the conviction that the other had led an unholy life, and Gabriel is not anxious for Florence to spend time with his wife (whom he also believes has also led an unholy life) or to be around his children whom he believes Florence will contaminate.

Literary Device

Florence and Elizabeth are character foils, enabling the reader to see how different experiences can lead two people in similar circumstances to perceive and react to their similar situations in different ways. They also serve to illustrate that those same people often find themselves in very similar positions despite different backgrounds. Elizabeth changed drastically (and for the worse) between the time when she was living with her parents and when the reader encounters her in her marriage with Gabriel.

The reader is made aware of these changes in Elizabeth by the narrator's descriptions of her, and her son, John's, observations of her. In her father's presence, for example, Elizabeth "pranced and postured like a very queen: and she was not afraid of anything," but John sees his mother with "dark hard lines running downward from her eyes, and the deep perpetual scowl in her forehead, and the down turned tightened mouth." He had seen a photograph of her once where she looked young and proud as if she knew no evil and was able to laugh. But the Elizabeth John knows never laughs, and he wonders how his mother had come to change so dramatically. John knows little about his mother and her hardships in her life and, therefore, cannot understand how such a change could have occurred.

The reader, on the other hand, is allowed into the entirety of Elizabeth's life and understands the events that have so changed her. It is through three separate, tragic events that Elizabeth changes. These events are significant not only in their own rite but also because they serve to illustrate how Elizabeth's separation from her father was an ongoing process, not just an immediate change in location, but a mental detachment and, finally, an ideological break as well.

The first blow to Elizabeth was her separation from her father— a relationship of love—and the consequent exile to the home of her aunt where her aunt, citing Elizabeth's pride as the causal factor, constantly prophesied Elizabeth's fall from grace. Living in her aunt's home was not just distasteful to Elizabeth, it was abhorrent. The reader knows almost nothing else of her time spent there. The aunt remains nameless, referred to only as "her aunt" or "she." During this first and most obvious separation from her father, which Elizabeth was forced to endure and in which she was physically removed from her father's side by her dead mother's sister and taken to live a great distance away, reunions with her father were few, and Elizabeth waited for him to come and take her away from her aunt as he had promised, but that long-awaited event never occurred.

The second event that jarred Elizabeth into a new world was the suicide of Richard because it was after his death that she was forced to become an adult: "Elizabeth, overnight, had become an old woman. . . ." Alone and pregnant, the young Elizabeth moved out of the home where she had been a border and found a squalid apartment of her own. This was the first time that she had lived away from family. First she was with her parents; then she was removed to her aunt's home; and then she was in the home of her aunt's relative. The diminishing consanguinity is indicative of the mental development into adulthood.

After Richard's death, Elizabeth found herself very lonely. She stopped associating with his friends because it was obvious that they had nothing in common and also because she didn't want them to know of Richard's child. She did not confide in her aunt; she was ashamed of her condition and could not go to her father for help because "she could not think of how to tell him, how to bring such pain to him who had had such pain already." Here the reader can see Elizabeth's quandary and mental separation from her father. That she was unable to think of a way to reach out to someone with whom she shared such a deep love shows that Elizabeth no longer knew her father and probably feared that he no longer knew her either.

After John's birth, Elizabeth saw almost no one and shunned the company of her coworkers. It was only Florence who was able to break Elizabeth's shell and befriend her. Perhaps, if she had had a greater network of friends or the help of her family, Elizabeth's life would have been much different. The loss of Richard separated Elizabeth from any support that could have given her strength. This tragedy set the stage for the next calamity in her life: her marriage to Gabriel.

When Elizabeth met Gabriel, she believed it to be a blessing for her; it turned out to be a bane. Elizabeth ignored her own fears when she first met Gabriel, the brother of her only friend, and entered into a relationship with him. She also ignored Florence's council against the union because Florence cited instances of his evildoings. Elizabeth relied on Gabriel for her strength, giving up her own self-sufficiency. Only after her marriage did Elizabeth discover the Gabriel that his sister hated. During their marriage, Elizabeth allowed herself and her children to be beaten by Gabriel, which is in direct opposition to her father's advice. Her father told her long ago, "if one had to die, to go ahead and die, but never let oneself be beaten." She endures her husband's rage because she has exchanged the pride that had carried her through her past trials for his empty promise of love. She is unable to stand up against her husband's brutality just as she is unable to leave him. That she has ignored her father's good advice proves that she has lost her final tie with him. She abandoned his ideology.

Glossary

stable   the group of women who work in a brothel, a house of prostitution.

chambermaid   a woman whose work is taking care of bedrooms, as in a hotel.

elevator boy   a man whose job it is to operate elevators which have to be manually controlled.

pearl without price   Elizabeth's aunt uses this metaphor to refer to Elizabeth's virginity.

sleep-in job   a job in which the worker is provided with room and board on the premises, as in the case of a live-in maid.

Gramophone   a phonograph, a device for reproducing sound that has been mechanically transcribed in a spiral groove on a circular disc or cylinder. A record player.

Moonshine   whiskey unlawfully distilled: often such whiskey made from corn and not matured in barrels.

Part Three: The Threshing Floor

Summary

Without knowing how it happens, John finds that he is lying on the floor of the church, and he feels something foreign possess his body. He is filled with a bitter anguish, and an evil voice tells him to rise and leave the church forever, but John finds that he cannot rise; instead, he feels himself falling away from the light.

John sees Gabriel looking at him with hatred and recalls that he had seen Gabriel naked, just as Noah's son had seen his father naked, and John wonders whether he, too, would be cursed as his predecessor had been. John then experiences several visions culminating in his journey to a river and a glimpse of God. John is saved, and he opens his eyes to the light of a new morning. He realizes that these people who surround him are protected by God just as he is now, and Elisha calls out to John to tell of his experience.

John finds himself unable to speak because of the joy that fills him, and the congregation begins to sing for him and his new found salvation. He knows he is an equal among the others, and when he finds himself in front of his mother, she says how proud she is of him. Gabriel, on the other hand, is stony faced while John searches for words that will bring the two of them together. He quotes part of Gabriel's own sermon of salvation to him, but Gabriel is unconvinced and unmoved. Florence ends the standoff between the two men by embracing John.

The churchgoers move out into the dirty streets and head for home in small groups. The older women discuss the events of the service and congratulate Elizabeth. They interpret her tears to be proof of her happiness and pride. They are not. Elizabeth is crying for John and the trials that he must face and for her lost love, John's biological father, Richard.

While Elizabeth talks to the other women, Florence speaks with Gabriel about John's salvation and future. She brings up the death of Ester and tells Gabriel that he can't fool God the way that he fools mortal men. Florence brings out Deborah's letter, which she has had for years and which tells of Deborah's suspicions of Royal's paternity.

Florence then chastises Gabriel for his treatment of the dead woman. Gabriel counters that he has sought and received forgiveness, and it is not Florence's place to pass judgment on him. Florence promises that before she dies she will make the truth known to Elizabeth so that Elizabeth will know that she is not the only one who has sinned and that John is not the only illegitimate child.

Walking down the street where he grew up, John sees that it is different than it was before his religious conversion and knows that it will never be the same. The same people are there and the same things happen, but *he* is different. He is free. He begins to cry again. Elisha gives him words of encouragement and admits, after John asks, that it was he, Elisha, who leaned over the suffering John and prayed for him. Elisha tells John that salvation is a constant and difficult struggle, but one need only to call upon Jesus for help. John asks Elisha to pray for him.

Everyone says their good-byes and separates until Sunday morning service. John turns and smiles at Gabriel who does not smile back. And then John speaks, "I'm ready. I'm coming. I'm on my way."

Commentary

Elisha plays an important role in this part of the book. John has resisted religion for so long because he believes that it would be Gabriel who would act as his intermediary to God. Instead, it is Elisha who stands in Gabriel's place beside John, helping him through his ordeal. It is Elisha whom John first sees upon opening his eyes after his visions. It is Elisha who helps John up from the threshing floor while Gabriel refuses to acknowledge that his stepson is saved. It is Elisha who rejoices that John has been reborn while Gabriel resents the fact that it is his stepson and not his son who has been redeemed.

Gabriel parents through power, not through love or example. When Florence asks Gabriel if he will help John live a holy life, Gabriel does not respond as one might expect a loving father to. Gabriel can only react to situations as they pertain to him: "The Lord done put his soul in *my* charge—and I ain't going to have that boy's blood on my hands." His sullen, authoritarian answer is "I am going to see to it. . . ." Gabriel is loath to help John on his journey of righteousness.

Elisha, on the other hand, rejoices for John and the opportunity to help him. He reassures John that, "I ain't going to stop praying for the brother what the Lord done give me." He cements their brotherhood with a "holy kiss" to John's forehead. Elisha promises to be something that Gabriel never has been and never will be: a positive role model who leads through example.

Literary Device

John's recollection of the story of Ham reflects his concern that he is cursed for having seen Gabriel naked and alludes to the often-cited biblical justification for slavery. The biblical Ham was the youngest son of Noah. After the great flood, Noah planted a vineyard, made wine, and became drunk. He fell asleep naked in his tent. Ham saw his father and mockingly told his brothers. Unlike Ham, his brothers—good sons—walked backwards into the tent which housed their father. Not looking at his nudity, the two brothers covered their father and departed. When Noah awoke and learned what had happened, he cursed Ham and Ham's descendants to be the slaves of his filial brothers ("servants of servants"). In a meager attempt to justify slavery biblically and morally, some contended that the Africans used as American slaves were descendants of Ham. No doubt Baldwin intends both of these references.

John realizes that time doesn't worry itself with curses. A curse is reborn every moment and given from a father to his son. It does seem, however, as though John has been cursed with at least part of Gabriel's attitude. When John stands at the top of a hill in Central Park, "he felt like a tyrant" and a "conqueror" that he would be "the most beloved, the Lord's anointed." Gabriel felt the same way on the morning of his own conversion. "He wanted power—he wanted to know himself to be the Lord's anointed . . . He wanted to be master. . . ."

The order is changed but the sentiment is the same. Both young men had a desire for power and a Holy position. Gabriel has been consumed by his distorted view of religion and has hurt those closest to him through his insistence on his absolute supremacy. It is certain that John does not want to inherit his father's ways. Perhaps Florence said it best when she tells Gabriel that his children are "going to do their best to keep it (his life) from becoming their lives."

Literary Device

In the church, just as in his home, John is surrounded by dirt. Though he and Elisha just finished sweeping and mopping the floor, it is still dirty. Here the dirt represents sin and corruption, and no amount of soap and water can wash those away. John finds himself lying on the "filthy" floor and "going farther and farther from the joy, the singing and the light above him." Above him is the church and beyond that heaven, below him the dirty floor and past that hell. John finds that the dust which is "sharp as the fumes of Hell" causes him "to cough and wretch," and he struggles to rise only to find that his body will not obey him. It is not his body that John must have charge of, it is his soul. His body obeys him only after his terrible visions and his glimpse of the Lord. It is then that John cries out to be saved and his new life begins.

John must struggle on the threshing floor to be saved from hell. He must ask God to raise him out of the dirt and into the holy light. Just as a baptism washes away sin, John is only able to come through his ordeal after his tears "sprang as from a mountain." His tears wash away his sin so that he is able to rise up from the dirty floor, purified and renewed for the kingdom of Heaven.

There is no real sense of closure in this novel. Each of the main characters (John, Gabriel, Elizabeth, and Florence) must come to an understanding of and make peace with not only each of the other characters but also themselves, including their decisions and their pasts. Although John attains salvation and a new outlook on life, he is still just embarking on his road to understanding. In the final pages, John does not suddenly become a self-actualized and content man; he is still a youth who is searching for happiness. He has just been shown the road that he must follow, and it is a long road. Elisha's final words to John echo this truth. He says to the boy, "Run on, little brother. Don't you get weary."

Elisha knows from personal experience that salvation does not come in one great blinding experience, but that it is a daily struggle. John himself seems to have a glimpse of the road ahead of him as witnessed by his final words: "I'm ready. I'm coming. I'm on my way." Perhaps he doesn't understand the depth of his struggle, but he does realize that there is a struggle ahead of him.

Elizabeth's future looks just as bleak as it did in the first pages of the novel. She has undergone no epiphany that has allowed her to take her life back into her own hands, and her past is still a weight that anchors her to sorrow. As the saints leave the church and begin their way home, the other women in the church misinterpret Elizabeth's tears as those for her son and his rebirth in the church. Instead, Elizabeth weeps for her lost Richard and the happiness and love that died with him. She has undergone no change by the end of the novel. Our last glimpse of her is as she "stood in the doorway, in the long shadows of the hall." She will never regain her pride and self-confidence, just as she will never cross the figurative threshold of Gabriel's dominance and come into her own light. She will live forever in the shadow of Gabriel.

Gabriel is just as self-righteous as he was in the beginning, dismissing his sister's admonishment of his hypocrisy with "I done answered already before my God. I ain't got to answer now, in front of you." He refuses to admit any guilt when confronted by Florence with his dead wife's letter. He doesn't deny that he had a child with Ester, but neither does he admit any remorse over the event. His feelings for his stepson have changed only in degree but not in kind. Gabriel still refuses to accept John and is not gladdened by John's conversion. He continues to treat John with a mixture of repugnance and disdain. His contempt of the boy has only been heightened in reaction to John's religious experience. He fails to accept John as holy, still insisting that it is the rebellious and angry Roy who will one day be lifted up to a place of honor in the church. Gabriel looks at John as having usurped Roy's rightful place in the kingdom of heaven. Gabriel believes that salvation is Roy's birthright, as he was born into a sanctified union, not John's, as he was born out of wedlock. Instead of bringing the two of them closer, John's experience seems to have had just the opposite effect. Gabriel is even more resentful of John than ever.

Florence sees this renewed tension in Gabriel and uses her only weapon—the letter—to protect John from his stepfather's unholy wrath. She has carried Deborah's letter for 30 years, never telling anyone but her husband of the damning contents. She exposes the letter now in an attempt to blackmail Gabriel on John's behalf. She makes Gabriel, and only Gabriel, aware that she knows the truth. Florence hopes that out of fear of exposure, Gabriel will not torment her nephew with renewed animosity.

Character Insight

Nor is there any change in Florence's character by the end of the novel. Florence still detests her brother and is still waiting to see him humiliated and exposed for his sins. She, however, is unlike the other characters because she doesn't lie to herself about her life. She may have a distorted image of the past and her place in it, but she does not ignore facts. Gabriel says to her, "You ain't never changed. You still waiting to see my downfall. You just as wicked now as you was when you was young." Florence doesn't deny his statement, she just elaborates on it. "No, I ain't changed. You ain't changed neither." Florence is a fatalist. She not only doesn't dispute that she has not changed; she has no expectations to do so in the future. She fully believes that with her impending death she will go to hell, but makes no effort to change her behavior.

Baldwin gives the reader no ending to the struggles of Gabriel, Elizabeth, and Florence, and for John he only gives us a new beginning. None of John's family members have found any solutions for their disagreements or found any way to end their strife. They are all the same people, living their same lives with the same problems they had at the onset of the novel. Florence says it best when she tells Deborah, "I reckon the Lord done give them *those* hearts—and honey, the lord don't give out no second helpings. . . ."

Glossary

threshing floor   Traditionally an area in which grain is beaten from its husks; here it is an area in the church where the saints pray. Metaphorically, it represents separating the sinners and the saved, just as the chaff is separated from wheat and is an allusion to the biblical passage, "His [God's] winnowing fork is in his hand, and he will clear his threshing floor, gathering his wheat into the barn and burning up the chaff with unquenchable fire (Matthew 3:12)."

ineffaceable   impossible to wipe out or erase.

Shadrach, Meshach, Abednego   the three biblical captives who came out of the fiery furnace miraculously unharmed: Daniel 3:12–27.

David   the biblical king of Israel and Judah, reputed to be the writer of many Psalms.

Jeremiah   a biblical prophet of the seventh and sixth centuries b.c.

the accursed son of Noah   Ham, who had laughed at his father's nudity and who had been cursed by his father to be "a servant of servants shall he be unto his brethren" (Genesis 9:18–27).

CHARACTER ANALYSES

John

John is the major character in the primary action (plot) of the story that spans about a 24-hour period from the time he awakens on a Saturday morning in March, 1935—his 14th birthday—to about dawn Sunday morning after he has "been saved." John is going through a very difficult time in his life. As if adolescence alone were not traumatic enough, he is confronted by a number of other dilemmas. First and most important in John's life and in the novel is his relationship with his father, Gabriel, who appears to harbor some sort of hostility toward John. The reasons for Gabriel's hostility have little or nothing to do with John; rather they are prejudices based on Gabriel's own past experiences and regrets that he projects on to John. Finally, although John does not know it, Gabriel is not his biological father.

The familial "sleight of hand" (first Gabriel is John's father, then he is not) not withstanding, Gabriel *is*, in every way but biological, John's father. He may not be the ideal, the best, or even a good father, but, by every standard we use to define fatherhood, save biological, Gabriel qualifies as, and John believes Gabriel to be, his father. Thematically, however, to whatever extent "the boy is father to the man," we are made aware, through John, of the potential that was likely once Gabriel's. John represents the potential man of subordinate status in the racist society of 1930s America (the setting of the novel) and, indeed, even 1950s America (when Baldwin published the work).

John does what he can to avoid what he perceives as his father's tyranny, and, when he realizes that his father will never be able to control him completely because he is reputed to have a good mind, John happily rationalizes that his intellect will someday lead him from his father's house. John is also bewildered by his lack of understanding of the biological (especially sexual) changes that are happening to him.

At this point in John's life, he does not endorse Gabriel's thinking related to matters of race, but the reader knows that John has many more years to accumulate knowledge based on experience before he will be in the position intellectually to challenge Gabriel's racial experiences, attitudes, and conclusions. Regretfully, however, there are already a few brief, but troubling and foreboding, references to John's unfortunate belief in the possibility that his own racial heritage is somehow inferior to that of whites. Nevertheless, at this juncture in his life, his overall attitudes toward race are much more optimistic if not more positive than Gabriel's.

Gabriel

At first glance, Gabriel is easy to dislike and easier yet to misinterpret. When the reader is introduced to Gabriel, he remains unnamed through the descriptive perspectives of his children, John, Roy, and Sara, and his wife, Elizabeth. We discover that Gabriel apparently endorses the popular, biblical notion of family structure at that time which dictated that the male has the power in the family. Gabriel interprets the father's role as *protector*: to feed, to clothe, to provide shelter, and to insure the holy status of his family's souls even if he must beat them into compliance. Any deed he does not approve he quickly classifies as wicked or sinful and, therefore, prohibited. In all matters, he holds his family's will subservient to his own. Disputes with his wife or children are often resolved by physical violence which he believes is not only condoned but mandated by God, and he enjoys his position as reverend, even though John views him as merely a "holy handyman" who is called upon when no one else is available.

Our first impression of Gabriel, however, is brought into question when, several pages into Part One, after we have just begun to solidify our judgment of him, we learn his name is Gabriel, an obvious allusion to the biblical Gabriel who was the prince of angels sent by God to make arrangements for the arrival of Jesus: Gabriel is the angel who informed Mary that she would give birth to the "Son of God" and probably the angel who was sent to Joseph and the shepherds; he is also the angel who earlier had informed Zacharias that he and his wife Elisabeth [sic] would parent John the Baptist.

Gabriel is an extremely important character in the novel, albeit not a complex one; he is more symbolic than realistic, and as such his character may appear to be flat and somewhat static because the reader does not see many sides to him, and he does not seem to change much throughout the novel. In terms of plot, Gabriel affects every character in the book. He is the unifying element that they all have in common. Thematically, Gabriel symbolizes first generation African Americans of former-slave parents, born free; therefore, he exhibits the heinous effects that the American slavery experience had on the generations of victims that followed the emancipation, the war, and the reconstruction periods.

Baldwin informs us of the biographical specifics that fashion Gabriel's character through descriptions of his impact on and relationships with the other characters—both past and present—throughout the novel. The reader is encouraged to pay particular attention to

"Part II: The Prayers of the Saints" in which Baldwin uses the flashback technique to fill in needed biological and historic data generally and to give the reader insights into Gabriel's psyche and motives through Florence, his sister; Elizabeth, his present wife; and Gabriel himself.

We learn that most importantly Gabriel is, as we all are, the product of his environment(s) and his experiences: He is all of the potential he possessed in youth percolated through a lifetime of hate and hostility, of unfulfilled ambitions and dreams, of unrealized hopes and expectations, of heartbreak and humiliation, of being demeaned and devalued. In short, he is a product of a lifetime of being a black man in a racist America. The reality of Gabriel's situation was that no matter how his mother may have endowed him, no matter what great qualities he may or may not have acquired or had bestowed upon him, his life options, his opportunities for the future, his very existence—whether he lived or died and how and when—were dictated, not by ambition or by intellect or by sacrifice or by hard work or by good deeds or by perseverance or even, at last, by prayer; instead they were dictated by the color and hue of his skin. He could have success and a successful life, but only with the permission of and within the parameters set by the white establishment and systems.

This sort of oppression creates in individuals, as it does in Gabriel, a strange combination of contradictory expectations, values, and behaviors; a situation in which a behavior does not actually demonstrate a value typically or ostensibly associated with it. As a young adult, for example, Gabriel's wild nights were undertaken in an apparent spirit of self-indulgence, as much as one can be self-indulgent and oppressed at the same time. Again, his refusal to take responsibility for his actions appears to be another of Gabriel's conspicuous characteristics; for example, he sees the short affair with Ester and her subsequent pregnancy as a consequence of *her* manipulating *him*. He rationalizes that she is an evil woman, a "harlot" who tempted him, "the Lord's anointed." Ester, of course, tells a different tale of the days leading up to their liaison. Gabriel, however, refuses to consider his own actions as being as culpable as Ester's, and he makes an adamant argument for his positions.

In order to understand Gabriel's apparently flawed rationale, one must be capable of understanding how an individual—or, for that matter, a whole race—develops and practices responsibility absent power and authority as this generation of African Americans was required to do. Gabriel's argument makes as much sense—is as reasonable and logical—as most of the arguments that control him and the world in which he exists.

One way of reconciling such apparent contradictions is to reorder the context within which they are rationalized. One context within which the whole racist environment could in any way make sense to a sane, rational, Christian people, was that it was some sort of divine test of the soul's mettle. The ability to cope with and to survive the subjugation and persecution without destroying one's faith or damaging one's soul becomes requisite to a better life after death, making religion and the religious life both the test and the reward. As a young man, Gabriel became a popular, much respected minister in the South, and his reputation and position in the church were enhanced rather than diminished by his past. He would not have been so powerful if he had not lived such a wild life. Had he always been devout, no one would have thought much of his service in the church, but converting from a life of wickedness made his position all the more remarkable.

All in all, Gabriel has few redeeming qualities. He shuns his responsibilities; he abuses his wife and children; he is arrogant; he lacks empathy with others; and he lacks courage to live the good life of which he is fully cognizant. His lack of character as the reader sees him is mitigated only by his experiences with American racism, which seems to have produced him.

Elizabeth

Elizabeth has suffered many heartaches. These heartaches, more than the joy in her life, have shaped who she is. First, she is taken from her loving father by her maternal aunt after Elizabeth's mother died. Then her lover—and the father of her unborn child—kills himself. The final calamity in Elizabeth's life is her marriage to Gabriel, an abusive and controlling husband and father.

Elizabeth's father was an open, loving man who cherished his daughter and delighted in her company. Elizabeth's view of her father may not have been the clearest view of him (he, for example, ran a house of prostitution); nevertheless, it is her perception of him that is important. With him, for example, she "pranced and postured like a very queen: and she was not afraid of anything." Elizabeth's aunt, who removed Elizabeth from her father's house, although she may have been justified in her actions, earned Elizabeth's undying hate for having done so. In addition, there is some evidence that the aunt was, at least occasionally, emotionally cruel to Elizabeth, castigating Elizabeth for her pride.

Elizabeth's relationship with Richard was also a loving relationship and one that resulted in her pregnancy. For Richard, Elizabeth acted as a sort of emotional buoy. Even though their marriage was somewhere in the indefinite future and Elizabeth was not comfortable with Richard's godless ways (he drank, for example), "She did not leave him, because, she was afraid of what might happen to him without her. She did not resist him, because he needed her." Still, in the end she was powerless to save him from false accusations and police brutality that brought about his suicide.

Her marriage to Gabriel was based on hope that quickly disintegrated. When he courted her, she saw him more as she wanted him to be than he really was. Elizabeth initially viewed Gabriel's strength—which later turned into domination—as salvation, thinking that he could redeem her and again make her a woman worthy of being a wife. Instead, Elizabeth finds herself with a physically and verbally abusive husband, someone more to be feared than loved. Her son John sees her now as a woman who never laughs and who has "dark hard lines running downward from her eyes, and the deep perpetual scowl in her forehead, and the down turned tightened mouth"—a far different description than the prancing girl who postured like a queen.

To her children, Elizabeth is a trusted and loving caregiver, but something of an enigma, especially to John. He understands that she speaks in a code that he does not understand; he also knows that her words have more meaning to her than they convey. Roy enjoys the arguments that he and his mother share over the breakfast table when his father is not home, but he does not understand why he can speak openly about his feelings with his mother but not with his father. That Elizabeth loves her children is obvious, but what is equally obvious is that, resigned to her life as she is, she is powerless to protect them.

The events that shape her character are significant not only in their own rite but also because they serve to illustrate how Elizabeth's separation from her father was an ongoing process, not just an immediate change in location, but a mental detachment and, finally, an ideological break as well. Her father had told her, "if one had to die, to go ahead and die, but never let oneself be beaten." But Elizabeth has been beaten—and beaten down.

Florence

Florence can perhaps be best described as thwarted. She has suffered disappointment and frustration that she has been unable to overcome and put behind her. Her familiarity with defeat has resulted in her a deep sense of helplessness and a desire for power.

The first and most devastating blow came with the birth of Gabriel. Instantly, from Florence's view, Gabriel, their mother's favorite, was given everything that their mother could afford at the expense of Florence. When new clothes and good food were available, they went to Gabriel. The opportunity for an education went to Gabriel even though he did not want to go to school, and Florence did. Florence—powerless to make any change in her situation—watched in silent rage as Gabriel squandered away the opportunities that Florence so desperately wanted for herself.

Even as an old and dying woman, Florence is unable to overcome her dislike for her brother. She does not believe that he has changed at all, even though he claims that he was saved and has become a respected preacher. Her belief is not unfounded. She knows about his affair with Ester and the child who was a result of the liaison. Other than Gabriel, she is the only living character aware of his indiscretion, and she keeps that knowledge and Deborah's letter to herself, waiting for an opportunity to make her brother suffer for his hypocrisy.

Knowledge of Royal's existence adds fuel to the fire of Florence's disdain for her brother and her belief in his hypocrisy, and her antipathy is destroying her soul just as her illness is destroying her body. The reader, however, is left with little conviction that Florence will actually use her proof against Gabriel. For so long, events have worked against her, and she inwardly doubts her own power to bring about any change. She clings to the promise of her brother's humiliation that the letter gives her as a woman desperate for something in which to believe.

The second disappointment in Florence's life is her failed relationship with Frank. Desperate for a measure of power in her life which she had for so long been denied, Florence married Frank out of the mistaken belief that she could change (control) him. She eventually discovered that she was unable to bend Frank into the man she truly wanted. It is after she comes to this realization that he leaves her.

Throughout the novel, Florence is motivated by a search for power and a sense of control. As a young woman, she left her home and family to travel north and make her own life. As a young woman, she was strong enough to recognize that she did not want the life that awaited her in the South and to make the effort to change her fate, even though doing so meant leaving behind everything familiar to her.

After her break with Frank, Florence is able to support herself and later to help Elizabeth through her trials. Most importantly, Florence is the only character to exhibit any power over the nearly omnipotent Gabriel. In the scene following the stabbing of Roy, Florence talks back to her brother without fear. It is also she who ends the beating of Roy by grabbing the belt Gabriel uses to whip him. Ironically, Florence already has the power she seeks; she just does not recognize it. And until she does, she will remain powerless.

Ester

Ester is a Hedonist: She does as she chooses when she chooses. She is unfettered by notions of sin and shame and is unconcerned with what others may think of her. She is an attractive young woman with many boyfriends who enjoys her employer's whiskey but not regular church attendance. It is a combination of these factors that initially draws Gabriel to her.

Ester's free and easy ways remind the reader of the young Gabriel before his conversion. Gabriel, for a short time, is able to live his old life again through his relationship with Ester. He is unwilling, however, to join her permanently in her "sinful" lifestyle, electing to return to his joyless marriage to Deborah and his life as a respected member of the community. Gabriel the Reverend condemns Ester for the lifestyle that he himself had once led. That he is attracted to Ester demonstrates that he is still attracted to his old ways.

Pride is another characteristic of the young woman. She is angry when Gabriel breaks off their affair but she does not argue with him in an attempt to prolong the relationship. Although she has had a number of previous boyfriends, she is insulted when Gabriel questions whether the unborn child is his. She may have a different moral code than Gabriel, but she lives by that code more consistently than Gabriel is able to follow his own.

Ester's pride also makes her unwilling to let the townspeople discover her condition. She is not ashamed but simply reluctant for her "mamma and daddy to know what a fool [she had] been." Although not ashamed of herself, she is ashamed of Gabriel and his response. He has hurt her pride and caused her to feel degraded and common. Ester is not a stupid woman. She knows Gabriel and his weaknesses and is able to use those against him to extort money for her trip to Chicago.

Gabriel's pride and self importance preclude the possibility that he could allow the townspeople to know that a "harlot" is carrying the child of "the Lord's anointed." Ester is, by this point, well aware of what Gabriel thinks of her and uses his opinion of her to her own advantage.

Royal

Royal is like his mother, Ester, and his father, Gabriel, in his younger days. He is not concerned with churchgoing and giving up earthly pleasures. He is motivated solely by his own desires. Never is he seen to act with any responsibility. The only time he does attempt to act in benefit of a cause outside of himself is when he tries to join the army; however, he is prevented from joining by his grandmother.

Even after his death, Royal continues to be an important character in the novel, affecting the lives of others who know nothing of him. Gabriel cannot accept the fact that it is his illegitimate stepson, John, and not his biological children (Royal or Roy), who is active in the church. Gabriel punishes the unwitting and bewildered child for taking the rightful place of his own sons, a place that neither son had or has any interest in. Gabriel finds it inconceivable and infuriating that John would be saved while his other sons are lost. Royal is literally lost to the grave, while the young and willful Roy seems to be lost to the dangerous lifestyle that his father escaped and that claimed the life of his half-brother. Elizabeth is not safe from Gabriel's memories of Royal either. When she unwittingly reminds Gabriel of his first son's death from a stab wound, Gabriel strikes her and knocks her to the floor.

Memories of Royal serve as a constant reminder to Gabriel of his own fallibility and potential for sin. Reminders of Royal also fuel Gabriel's guilt for fathering a child but not raising him, allowing him to go off by himself and be killed. Royal's ghost is omnipresent in the Grimes household, acting as a barrier between Gabriel and his family, a barrier that prevents real communication, honesty, and acceptance among those who should be close to one another.

Richard

Richard is another character who is very proud. Unlike Ester, whose pride is a source of strength, Richard's pride makes him emotionally vulnerable. Initially Richard's pride leads him to educate himself so that no one would ever be able to insult him or embarrass him because of his ignorance. This was no easy task because he received little education as a child. His mother had died when he was young and his father was absent, so he was passed around among relatives until he was old enough to fend for himself. As an adult, Richard enjoys visiting museums and reading about a variety of subjects. He also takes classes while he works.

Richard's situation serves as a kind of microcosm of the general theme of the novel. Richard is an admirable, noble character who has no apparent character flaws, who does as the dominant (white) society would have him do in his situation, and who works hard to improve himself. Richard's greatest fear is to loose his pride, to be humiliated to the degree that he felt it in his soul. His strategy is to fortify himself against such a possibility; therefore, he educates himself; he works hard; he performs his work well, and he offends no one. Nevertheless, by sheer coincidence, by a tragic, random act of fate, by simply being in the wrong place at the wrong time, but most importantly by being African-American, Richard is swept into the racist system by the very arm of that system whose responsibility it is to protect him. His character is irrelevant; his protestations of innocence are irrelevant; his history, his education, his employment record, his personality—all are irrelevant.

Richard is unable to withstand the blows to his pride. The racially motivated arrest along with the resulting racial slurs and physical abuse leave him emotionally devastated. Humiliated to his soul, he commits suicide.

CRITICAL ESSAYS

Racism

In *Go Tell It on the Mountain*, Baldwin depicts the insidious effects of systemic racism, producing for us a glimpse of the inhumanity that is the second and third generation result of the era of American slavery that took place virtually from the period of colonization through the American Civil War. The novel takes place in 1935, only 73 years after the signing of the Emancipation Proclamation (1862) and 70 years after Robert E. Lee surrendered to Ulysses S. Grant (April 1865), ending the American Civil War, and the ratification of the 13th Amendment abolishing slavery (December 1865). Thus, the novel's characters are only slightly removed (a generation or two) from their slave ancestors. We learn, for example, in Part Two, that Gabriel's and Florence's mother was a slave, freed only by the Emancipation Proclamation and the Civil War.

As a result of this proximity to slavery, the characters of the novel suffer a special set of physical, psychological, and social circumstances: Gabriel and Florence, for example, have siblings they will never know because, as property, their siblings were taken from their mother for various reasons (but all having to do with their slave—therefore, race—status and circumstances). The great migration north originally held promise of better times and circumstances for each character, but ultimately resulted in only a different, often more oppressive, level and manifestation of the racism they were attempting to escape.

These consequences of the American slave era and other vestiges of this period that survived the Proclamation and the War constitute the racism that Baldwin depicts in *Go Tell It on the Mountain*: It is second and third generation, slave-psyche racism, a racism based on the notion that one group of people is socially, genetically, and intentionally superior to another. This form of racism works its evil and malice on both the perpetrator and the victim. The processes and philosophies that enable and defend the subordination of one group of individuals to another, based on propagating and advocating artificial values and ethics for economic or status reasons, tend to infect both the victims and the victimizers.

Our very nature and culture cause us to defend what we do as morally right or definitely not wrong or, at least, morally neutral. Here and there, evil individuals may do evil things with the full knowledge that what they are doing is evil; however, most of us feel a need to convince ourselves—and, most often, others—that what we do is, at least, not wrong.

When issues of great magnitude for or against one population to the advantage or detriment of another population—especially when the outcome is to subordinate one group to another—are given a rationale in defense of their existence, that rationale, usually steeped in arrogance and insensitivity on the part of its proponents, establishes and propagates irrational delusions of righteousness and natural superiority coupled with false standards of value and ethics in both the superordinate and subordinate populations. These "delusions" of superiority are, in subsequent generations, generally accepted as moral or ethical truths.

It is the circumstance in which one has been taught and conditioned to believe and think a certain "something" without really examining or questioning it, without submitting that something to the scrutiny of logic or any other examination to determine its validity or truth. It is a kind of major premise, almost a cultural reflex, something we believe or say or do without really knowing why. Hence, at some point—in the American ethos that supported slavery—one or both populations may generally believe and endorse religious fabrications, such as the African-American blackness being the mark of Ham, or uphold distorted cultural values, such as lighter skin tones are "better" than darker skin tones. The victims of such thinking may adhere to *illusions* of freedom and power, such as those found in physical and sexual conquests; they may harbor diminished expectations or standards of success and satisfaction; or they may resort to any escape possible, either through opiates (such as alcohol) or exaggerated adherence to religion and religious activity.

Baldwin demonstrates this effect of racism in each of his major characters. Consider, for example, Florence's aversion to blackness; she uses skin whiteners (symbolic of self hatred), and she dislikes "common niggers," a symptom of a racist cataloguing within the race. Or consider the sadly casual explanation of how Rachel (Florence and Gabriel's mother) had lost her other children: ". . . all of whom had been taken from her, one by sickness, two by auction; and one, whom she had not been allowed to call her own, had been raised in the master's house."

In the two main characters, John and Gabriel, however, Baldwin shows the effects of racism most vividly. John is the central character in the main plot (the boy maturing physically and religiously); Gabriel figures most prominently in its major theme (the tragic effects of racism on a people and a society). Each is the product of his environment, and each reflects the debilitating nature and consequences of the racism in his environment.

The views of John and Gabriel regarding racism are polar opposites. John is still a child, naïve and inexperienced; Gabriel has suffered the realities of his subordinate position in a racist society; he is embittered, hardened, and defeated. While John recalls the kindness of a concerned teacher when he was sick, Gabriel can think only of injustices that African Americans endured where he grew up and where he lives.

Gabriel proclaims whites to be wicked and untrustworthy, warning John that, when he is older, he will find out for himself how evil they really are. John has read about racism and the injustices and tortures that blacks had endured in the South, but he has experienced none of these things himself. Because John has had no overt, negative experiences with whites, "it was hard for him to think of them burning in hell forever," as Gabriel promises they will.

John, of course, is not without racist attitudes, however. In fact, John illustrates the most tragic and insidious variety of racism: racism directed against ones own people and hence oneself. While disparaging the compliments of those of his own race, John revels in the fact that he has also been singled out for praise by whites. Baldwin writes "John was not much interested in his people . . ." and "It was not only colored people who praised John, since they could not, John felt, in any case really know." When his white school principal tells John that he is a "very bright boy," John sees a new life opening up, but when his neighbors tell him that he will be a great leader of his people, he is unmoved.

Oppression is always about power of some sort, and the power in *Mountain* appears to be heavily skewed in Gabriel's favor, particularly within his family and his church. In the larger context, however, in issues relating to having dominion, sovereignty, or control over one's life, Gabriel has been emasculated, an idea brought graphically to life by the powerful image of the castrated African-American soldier in "Gabriel's Prayer." Gabriel's dominance of family is an illustration of a diminished and distorted standard of power. Gabriel is the product of the racist environments in which he has existed from birth. He has suffered the anxiety and confusion of the Southern, newly freed, slave environment; anticipation and separation anxieties associated with the Great Migration; and the angst and ego-devastating environment of the Northern oppression and bigotry. Although not an excuse for his cruel behavior, it is an explanation for it. Gabriel cannot confront the society that marginalized him and give expression to his frustration and anger; thus he uses his family and the church as outlets for his emotions.

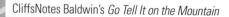

The Church

The importance of The Church of the Fire Baptized cannot be overstated. This church acts as an anchor for its members and promises them the riches of heaven when their poverty-filled lives end. It provides a community in which people can find support and guidance and share their trouble and their happiness with like-minded people. Moral guidelines are established and members are expected to live by them. In this way, it teaches its members the group morality and discourages destructive behavior.

The church is also an outlet for repressed emotions and energy. Violence is not a socially acceptable manner by which to cope with anger and frustration. Releasing those passions in church through singing, shouting, and clapping gives an acceptable release of pent-up emotion. Energy that could have turned into violence is expressed through prayer. However, there are drawbacks in The Church of the Fire Baptized. Its members tend to be rigid in their way of thinking and can be judgmental in their views of others. Proof of this can be found in what they call themselves. Members of the church are called "saints." If there are *saints*, then there must also be *sinners*, and the sinners appear to be everyone but themselves. Attending church fills them with a feeling of moral supremacy. At times it seems as though there is a contest to see who is the most holy and the most faithful in the church. Sister McCandles says of John, "This boy going to make it to the Kingdom before any of them," as if salvation is some kind of footrace where the winner gets a little trophy at the end.

It is significant that the church the Grimes family attends is a storefront church. It is significant partly because it is not a church; it is a storefront used as a church, an example of a diminished standard or expectation, a symbol of a people forced to use and be satisfied with that which others have discarded. A church can, of course, be any building or place where people come together to worship, but the fact the edifice in which the saints gather was not originally intended to be a church gives the reader a clue to the social status of the characters. They are poor and of a lower social class. The grand churches of the city are reserved for those who have more money and social status than they.

Gabriel has his first taste of hypocrisy in the church during the banquet following the Twenty-Four Elders revival meeting. The ministers are ostensibly the messengers of God, men who had forsaken worldly pleasures in order to serve God and their fellow man. In practice, however, they are much different. Gabriel finds them too well dressed and too well fed and more full of themselves than they are of the holy spirit. That these men of God mock Deborah and ridicule her rape repulses Gabriel.

Of course, Gabriel is not the model Christian either. He is a violent man who beats his wife and children. He has had an adulterous affair and has stolen money from his wife to keep a liaison a secret. He is also a hypocrite. He has dismissed his own affair with Ester as forgiven but refuses to allow Elizabeth the same courtesy. It is not surprising that the young John feels some ambivalence toward the church when the reality of the institution varies so widely from the ideal.

Homosexuality as a Subtext

John, at the age of 14, is in puberty. Bewildered by his "treacherous body" and all of the changes that he is going through, many things become sexual images. A stain on the ceiling above his bed suddenly takes on the shape of a naked woman. He had masturbated in the school lavatory while thinking of older boys and has "watched in himself a transformation of which he could never speak." Even his friend and Sunday school teacher, Elisha, has been eroticized. John has a difficult time concentrating during his Sunday morning lessons because he is distracted by the physical appearance of the older boy whom John believes to be "tall and handsome" and by the timbre of his voice which is "manlier than his own." John respects Elisha as his elder in the church, but he also admires his physical person as much as he admires his character.

Although John's feeling could very well belong to a young heterosexual male in puberty, it is also possible that they are John's emerging feelings of homosexuality, a subtle subtext that is never directly confronted but that is woven into the story. Baldwin does not state directly that John is gay, but there are many instances which suggest that he may be. Take, for example, the incident on the morning of his birthday, when John's thoughts turn to his "sin" of masturbating while thinking of the older boys. In addition to the anonymous boys whom John recalls in the lavatory, there seems to be one person for whom John has a special affinity. That is Elisha. We learn that John had a difficult time concentrating in Sunday school because he was distracted by the physical appearance, voice, and strength of Elisha. Baldwin eroticizes Elisha in the description of Elisha's ecstasy in church when he feels himself overcome by the power of the Holy Spirit. Elisha's head is "thrown back, eyes closed, sweat standing on his brow . . . he stiffened and cried out . . . It seemed that he could not breathe, that his body could not contain this passion . . . until he dropped . . . moaning, on his face." This description of holy rapture parallels sexual union in non-too subtle manner. We are seeing Elisha through John's eyes, and while John does respect Elisha as a teacher and minister, the reader sees (although John may not) that his admiration does not necessarily stop there.

That John's view of Elisha during this incident is more sexual than spiritual does not prove definitively that John is homosexual. Remember that he watched a couple in an abandoned building while they had sex and looked at Ella Mae in a less than saintly manner when she and Elisha were called before the congregation for "walking disorderly." Nevertheless, the possibility of John's emerging homosexuality adds nuances to his struggle to find a place for himself in his body, in his home, and in his life.

CliffsNotes Review

Use this CliffsNotes Review to test your understanding of the original text and reinforce what you've learned in this book. After you work through the review and essay questions, identify the quote section, and the fun and useful practice projects, you're well on your way to understanding a comprehensive and meaningful interpretation of *Go Tell It on the Mountain*.

Q&A

1. Where did Ester have her baby?

   a. at home

   b. in New York

   c. in Chicago

2. Where did Gabriel get the money he gave to Ester?

   a. he stole it from Deborah

   b. he earned it from preaching

   c. he borrowed it from his employer

3. Who are John's biological parents?

   a. Gabriel and Ester

   b. Gabriel and Elizabeth

   c. Elizabeth and Richard

4. Florence and Elizabeth first met each other

   a. at church

   b. at work

   c. grocery shopping

5. How did Richard die?

   a. he was stabbed in an argument about a card game

   b. he committed suicide

   c. he was beaten to death by white police officers

6. Elizabeth met Richard while he was working in a _____.

7. Roy's mother is _____ and his father is _____.

8. John chooses to spend his birthday money on a _____.

9. Gabriel first saw Royal at _____.

10. Elizabeth was introduced to Gabriel by _____.

Answers: (1) c. (2) a. (3) c. (4) b. (5) b. (6) store (7) Elizabeth, Gabriel (8) movie (9) Ester's funeral (10) Florence

Identify the Quote

1. I just don't want him beating on me all the time, I ain't no dog.

2. You're a very bright boy, John Grimes.

3. You slap her again, you black bastard, and I swear to God that I'll kill you.

4. Boy, ain't it time you was thinking about your soul?

5. Lord, sprinkle the doorpost of this house with the blood of the Lamb to keep all the wicked men away.

6. I hate him! I hate him! Big, black, prancing tomcat of a nigger!

7. Ma, I'm going. I'm a-going this morning.

8. All right, baby. I guess you don't never want to see me no more, not a miserable black sinner like me.

9. I ain't the first man been made to fall on account of a wicked woman.

10. I'm going to have my baby and I'm going to bring him up to be a man . . . . If he don't drink nothing but moonshine all his natural days he be a better man than his Daddy.

11. Gabriel . . . that Royal . . . he were your flesh and blood, weren't he?

12. I'm ready, I'm coming. I'm on my way.

Answers: (1) [Roy to Elizabeth, about Gabriel.] (2) [The school principal to John, encouraging him.] (3) [Roy to Gabriel, trying to protect Elizabeth.] (4) [Elisha to John, speaking as his friend and spiritual mentor.] (5) [Rachel in a prayer, asking that God keep white men away from their home.] (6) [Florence to Deborah, speaking about her brother, Gabriel] (7) [Florence to Rachel, telling her mother that she is leaving to go North.] (8) [Frank to Florence, when he leaves her.] (9) [Gabriel to Ester, casting the blame for their affair solely on Ester.] (10) [Ester in a letter to Gabriel, about the unborn Royal.] (11) [Deborah to Gabriel, questioning his relationship with Royal.] (12) [John to himself and Gabriel, after John's religious experience in the church.]

Essay Questions

1. Deborah is often described as unattractive. What is the source of her unattractiveness? Examine how her reaction to the rape and the townspeople's reaction could explain this description.

2. Discuss whether Florence will use Deborah's letter to expose Gabriel's past. What would be possible outcomes or either scenario? What, if any, changes would occur in the lives of the characters?

3. What might Elizabeth's life have been like if her aunt had not taken her from her father or if Richard had not committed suicide?

4. Discuss the similarities and differences between Roy and Gabriel or between Roy and Royal.

5. What effect, if any, did the affair with Ester and the birth of Royal have on the life of Gabriel.

6. The novel ends without much resolution regarding the characters' dilemmas, leaving the door open for speculation on what will—or can—happen. Write what you believe will happen in the next chapter of the characters' lives. Base your thoughts on the personalities of the characters and what they are likely—or unlikely—to do.

7. Many different themes run through the novel. What do you see as the most important aspect of the book? Is it a coming of age story? Is it about religion, racism, families, or something else? Pull evidence from the book to substantiate your opinion.

Practice Projects

1. Create a Web site that introduces *Go Tell It on the Mountain* to other readers. Design pages to intrigue and inform your audience and invite other readers to post their thoughts and responses to their reading of the novel.

2. Write a sermon for Gabriel to give some Sunday. Using what you know of Gabriel's character, make sure that the text and the delivery represent Gabriel as Baldwin depicts him. Use, as best you can, his "voice."

3. Choose a scene from the novel and dramatize it for other classes. The production will require putting the scene in play form (freely adapted according to inspiration), assigning roles, directing, and staging the production. Follow the performance with a discussion of the novel's themes.

CliffsNotes Resource Center

The learning doesn't need to stop here. CliffsNotes Resource Center shows you the best of the best—links to the best information in print and online about the author and/or related works. And don't think that this is all we've prepared for you; we've put all kinds of pertinent information at www.cliffsnotes.com. Look for all the terrific resources at your favorite bookstore or local library and on the Internet. When you're online, make your first stop www.cliffsnotes.com where you'll find more incredibly useful information about *Go Tell It on the Mountain*.

Books

This CliffsNotes book provides a meaningful interpretation of *Go Tell It on the Mountain*. If you are looking for information about the author and/or related works, check out these other publications:

James Baldwin (Modern Critical Views), edited by Harold Bloom. This collection of essays features comparisons of some of Baldwin's best known works in addition to a variety of articles on various subjects. Included after the essays is a brief chronology of the events of Baldwin's life. New York: Chelsea House Publishers, 1986.

The Critical Reception of James Baldwin in France, by Rosa Bobia. This book gives a rare insight into the differences and similarities between the cultures to which Baldwin was drawn. In the reviews of his literature from another culture, the reader perceives a perspective different from what he or she may be accustomed to. New York: Peter Lang Publishing, 1997.

New Essays on Go Tell It on the Mountain, edited by Trudier Harris. This book offers a collection of essays from six different contributors, covering a variety of subjects and giving many different viewpoints. It is a great starting point for research topics and essay questions. It also includes a list of works cited after each article and a comprehensive bibliography. New York: Cambridge University Press, 1996.

Black Women in the Fiction of James Baldwin, by Trudier Harris, explores the women in Baldwin's novels. It is helpful because female characters are so often eclipsed by their male counterpart in the fiction of Baldwin and consequently in reviews of his work. By focusing on the women in the stories, Harris gives the reader a perspective that may have otherwise been missed. Knoxville: University of Tennessee Press, 1985.

James Baldwin: A Biography, by David Leeming. Written by a close friend of Baldwin, this biography tells the story of Baldwin's life as completely as is possible. Much of the material was gained from Baldwin himself and the reader is informed not only of the events that shaped the man's life but also his emotions and mindset during different times. Events leading up to the writing and publication of his works are explored in reference to how they influenced the author and his work. New York: Knopf, 1994.

Critical Essays on James Baldwin, edited by Fred L. Standley and Nancy V. Burt, is a comprehensive collection that covers a variety of subjects in Baldwin's fiction, nonfiction, and drama. It is a helpful reference for comparing similar themes in different genres. Boston: Gc.K. Hall, 1988.

It's easy to find books published by IDG Books Worldwide, Inc. You'll find them in your favorite bookstores (on the Internet and at a store near you). We also have three Web sites that you can use to read about all the books we publish:

- www.cliffsnotes.com
- www.dummies.com
- www.idgbooks.com

Internet

Check out these Web resources for more information about James Baldwin and *Go Tell It on the Mountain*:

Writing and Resistance, www.public.asu.edu/~metro/aflit/—An excellent site. At the time this was written, the site included 14 different African-American authors, each with a biography, a bibliography of works, and an exhaustive listing of literary criticism. Another helpful feature is a page of links to other sites that cover related topics.

NPR Online, www.talkofthenation@npr.org—At the NPR home page, complete a search by using the keyword "James Baldwin." Doing so leads you to an audio program featuring a Baldwin scholar and call-in guests discussing *Go Tell It on the Mountain*. It is an interesting program with perspectives from many different people who express viewpoints that may be new to you. Transcripts are available and may be ordered at the site.

Next time you're on the Internet, don't forget to drop by www.cliffsnotes.com. We created an online Resource Center that you can use today, tomorrow, and beyond.

Send Us Your Favorite Tips

In your quest for knowledge, have you ever experienced that sublime moment when you figure out a trick that saves time or trouble? Perhaps you realized you were taking ten steps to accomplish something that could have taken two. Or you found a little-known workaround that achieved great results. If you've discovered a useful resource that gave you insight into or helped you understand *Go Tell It on the Mountain* and you'd like to share it, the CliffsNotes staff would love to hear from you. Go to our Web site at www.cliffsnotes.com and click the Talk to Us button. If we select your tip, we may publish it as part of CliffsNotes Daily, our exciting, free e-mail newsletter. To find out more or to subscribe to a newsletter, go to www.cliffsnotes.com on the Web.

Index

NOTES

liffsNotes

LITERATURE NOTES

bsalom, Absalom!
he Aeneid
gamemnon
lice in Wonderland
ll the King's Men
ll the Pretty Horses
ll Quiet on the
  Western Front
ll's Well &
  Merry Wives
merican Poets of the
  20th Century
merican Tragedy
nimal Farm
nna Karenina
nthem
ntony and Cleopatra
ristotle's Ethics
As I Lay Dying
The Assistant
As You Like It
Atlas Shrugged
Autobiography of
  Ben Franklin
Autobiography of
  Malcolm X
The Awakening
Babbit
Bartleby & Benito
  Cereno
The Bean Trees
The Bear
The Bell Jar
Beloved
Beowulf
The Bible
Billy Budd & Typee
Black Boy
Black Like Me
Bleak House
Bless Me, Ultima
The Bluest Eye & Sula
Brave New World
Brothers Karamazov

The Call of the Wild &
  White Fang
Candide
The Canterbury Tales
Catch-22
Catcher in the Rye
The Chosen
The Color Purple
Comedy of Errors…
Connecticut Yankee
The Contender
The Count of
  Monte Cristo
Crime and Punishment
The Crucible
Cry, the Beloved
  Country
Cyrano de Bergerac
Daisy Miller &
  Turn…Screw
David Copperfield
Death of a Salesman
The Deerslayer
Diary of Anne Frank
Divine Comedy-I.
  Inferno
Divine Comedy-II.
  Purgatorio
Divine Comedy-III.
  Paradiso
Doctor Faustus
Dr. Jekyll and Mr. Hyde
Don Juan
Don Quixote
Dracula
Electra & Medea
Emerson's Essays
Emily Dickinson Poems
Emma
Ethan Frome
The Faerie Queene
Fahrenheit 451
Far from the Madding
  Crowd
A Farewell to Arms
Farewell to Manzanar
Fathers and Sons
Faulkner's Short Stories

Faust Pt. I & Pt. II
The Federalist
Flowers for Algernon
For Whom the Bell Tolls
The Fountainhead
Frankenstein
The French
  Lieutenant's Woman
The Giver
Glass Menagerie &
  Streetcar
Go Down, Moses
The Good Earth
The Grapes of Wrath
Great Expectations
The Great Gatsby
Greek Classics
Gulliver's Travels
Hamlet
The Handmaid's Tale
Hard Times
Heart of Darkness &
  Secret Sharer
Hemingway's
  Short Stories
Henry IV Part 1
Henry IV Part 2
Henry V
House Made of Dawn
The House of the
  Seven Gables
Huckleberry Finn
I Know Why the
  Caged Bird Sings
Ibsen's Plays I
Ibsen's Plays II
The Idiot
Idylls of the King
The Iliad
Incidents in the Life of
  a Slave Girl
Inherit the Wind
Invisible Man
Ivanhoe
Jane Eyre
Joseph Andrews
The Joy Luck Club
Jude the Obscure

Julius Caesar
The Jungle
Kafka's Short Stories
Keats & Shelley
The Killer Angels
King Lear
The Kitchen God's Wife
The Last of the
  Mohicans
Le Morte d'Arthur
Leaves of Grass
Les Miserables
A Lesson Before Dying
Light in August
The Light in the Forest
Lord Jim
Lord of the Flies
The Lord of the Rings
Lost Horizon
Lysistrata & Other
  Comedies
Macbeth
Madame Bovary
Main Street
The Mayor of
  Casterbridge
Measure for Measure
The Merchant
  of Venice
Middlemarch
A Midsummer Night's
  Dream
The Mill on the Floss
Moby-Dick
Moll Flanders
Mrs. Dalloway
Much Ado About
  Nothing
My Ántonia
Mythology
Narr. …Frederick
  Douglass
Native Son
New Testament
Night
1984
Notes from the
  Underground

CliffsNotes™

@ cliffsnotes.com

The Odyssey
Oedipus Trilogy
Of Human Bondage
Of Mice and Men
The Old Ma
the Sea
Old Testame
Oliver Twist
The Once ar
Future Kii
One Day in
Ivan Deni
One Flew O
Cuckoo's Nest
100 Years of Solitude
O'Neill's Plays
Othello
Our Town
The Outsiders
The Ox Bow Incident
Paradise Lost
A Passage to India
The Pearl
The Pickwick Papers
The Picture of
Dorian Gray
Pilgrim's Progress
The Plague
Plato's Euthyphro…
Plato's The Republic
Poe's Short Stories
A Portrait of the
Artist…
The Portrait of a Lady
The Power and
the Glory
Pride and Prejudice
The Prince
The Prince and
the Pauper
A Raisin in the Sun
The Red Badge of
Courage
The Red Pony
The Return of the
Native
Richard II
Richard III

The Rise of
Silas Lapham
Robinson Crusoe
Roman Classics
Shakespeare's Tragedies
Shaw's Pygmalion &
Arms…
Silas Marner
Sir Gawain…Green
Knight
Sister Carrie
Slaughterhouse-Five
Snow Falling on Cedars
Song of Solomon
Sons and Lovers
The Sound and the Fury
Steppenwolf &
Siddhartha
The Stranger
The Sun Also Rises
T.S. Eliot's Poems &
Plays
A Tale of Two Cities
The Taming of the
Shrew
Tartuffe, Misanthrope…
The Tempest
Tender Is the Night
Tess of the D'Urbervilles
Their Eyes Were
Watching God
Things Fall Apart
The Three Musketeers
To Kill a Mockingbird
Tom Jones
Tom Sawyer
Treasure Island &
Kidnapped
The Trial

Tristram Shandy
Troilus and Cressida
Twelfth Night

Who's Afraid of
Virginia…
Winesburg, Ohio
The Winter's Tale
The Woman Warrior
Worldly Philosophers
Wuthering Heights
A Yellow Raft in
Blue Water

Check Out the All-New CliffsNotes Guides

TECHNOLOGY TOPICS
Balancing Your Check-
book with Quicken
Buying and Selling
on eBay
Buying Your First PC
Creating a Winning
PowerPoint 2000
Presentation
Creating Web Pages
with HTML
Creating Your First
Web Page
Exploring the World
with Yahoo!
Getting on the Internet
Going Online with AOL
Making Windows 98
Work for You

Setting Up a
Windows 98
Home Network
Shopping Online Sa
Upgrading and
Repairing Your P
Using Your First iMa
Using Your First PC
Writing Your First
Computer Progra

PERSONAL FINANCE TOPIC
Budgeting & Saving
Your Money
Getting a Loan
Getting Out of Debt
Investing for the
First Time
Investing in
401(k) Plans
Investing in IRAs
Investing in
Mutual Funds
Investing in the
Stock Market
Managing Your Mone
Planning Your
Retirement
Understanding
Health Insurance
Understanding
Life Insurance

CAREER TOPICS
Delivering a Winning
Job Interview
Finding a Job
on the Web
Getting a Job
Writing a Great Resume